The Principal's Purpose

A Practical Guide to Moral and Ethical School Leadership

Leanna Stohr Isaacson

EYE ON EDUCATION
6 DEPOT WAY WEST, SUITE 106
LARCHMONT, NY 10538
(914) 833–0551
(914) 833–0761 fax
www.eyeoneducation.com

Library of Congress Cataloging-in-Publication Data

Isaacson, Leanna Stohr, 1939-
  The principal's purpose : a practical guide to moral and
ethical school leadership / Leanna Stohr Isaacson.
       p. cm.
  Includes bibliographical references.
  ISBN 1-59667-048-7
1. School principals—Professional ethics—United States.
2. Educational leadership—Moral and ethical aspects—
United States. 3. School management and organization—United
States. I. Title.
  LB2831.92.I828 2007
  371.2'012—dc22

                                        2007002428

10 9 8 7 6 5 4 3 2 1

Editorial and production services provided by
Hypertext Book and Journal Services
738 Saltillo St., San Antonio, TX 78207-6953 (210-227-6055)

Dealing with Difficult Teachers, Second Edition
Todd Whitaker

Dealing with Difficult Parents
(And with Parents in Difficult Situations)
Todd Whitaker and Douglas Fiore

Lead with Me:
A Principal's Guide to Teacher Leadership
Gayle Moller and Anita Pankake

Creating the High Schools of Our Choice
Tim Westerberg

Lead Me—I Dare You!
Managing Resistance to Change
Sherrel Bergmann and Judith Brough

Elevating Student Voice: How To Enhance
Participation, Citizenship, and Leadership
Nelson Beaudoin

Stepping Outside Your Comfort Zone:
Lessons for School Leaders
Nelson Beaudoin

What Great Teachers Do *Differently*:
14 Things That Matter Most
Todd Whitaker

Motivating & Inspiring Teachers
The Educational Leader's Guide for Building Staff Morale
Todd Whitaker, Beth Whitaker, and Dale Lumpa

Instructional Leadership for School Improvement
Sally J. Zepeda

Data Analysis for Continuous School Improvement
Victoria L. Bernhardt

Handbook on Teacher Evaluation:
Assessing and Improving Performance
James Stronge & Pamela Tucker

Table of Contents

Acknowledgments

I would like to thank my family, friends, principals, and college students who helped me formalize the practical application of concepts that deeply affect practicing school leaders. In addition, those who edited my work helped me clarify my thinking by asking the hard questions.

Bob Sickles, editor and publisher of Eye on Education, remains a constant supporter and encourager. His patience, understanding, and expertise kept me going through the process of writing about a practical application to a complex set of concepts.

I am indebted to my longtime friend, Dr. Lynn Erickson, popular author, international independent consultant, and one who continually stretches my brain, in the quest to develop higher-order conceptual thinking for adults and students. She took time from her demanding schedule to help me with suggestions for this manuscript and edit this work. Dr. Paula Whittier, national consultant, and writer also provided ideas to help the reader clarify each of the topics. She too took time from her busy schedule to provide invaluable suggestions for content and editing.

Kim Stutsman, principal and close personal friend, listens endlessly to my thoughts about ways to apply the identified critical concepts to the practical application in schools. Robbie McNabb, veteran principal, provides in-depth insight into the culture of schools. Our conversations cement the importance of establishing an environment of collaboration and focused attention when implementing the school mission, vision, values, and goals. Additional recognition goes to Vicki Roscoe, principal, and Ralph Hewitt, retired principal and consultant. They continue to remind me of our experiences as principals and the reality of the world of school leadership.

My Stetson University students in educational leadership classes provided field-testing opportunities for the identified concepts. As I observed them working through the process I realized the importance of training potential school administrators at the university level in the practical application of understanding moral, ethical, and purposeful leadership when developing school mission, vision, values, and goals.

The first line of conversation, suggestions, and editing begins with my son Greg. He sees issues from the perspective of a lawyer, and head of the English department of Olympia High School in Orlando, Florida, where he teaches. He provides insight and identifies issues surrounding high school administrators, teachers, and students. The impact of moral, ethical, and purposeful leadership on teachers and principals comes alive when listening to my grandson, Destin McMahon. He and his friends provide a thoughtful perspective through the eyes of middle and high school students. He translates teacher actions into student perception. My daughter Lara, his mom, provides insight into the world of educators from the perspective of a parent. Their questions become important points of reference. I am indebted to them for their patience and support.

I have a rare opportunity to return to the role of "recycled principal" in the upcoming months while the principal of my former school takes maternity leave. Then, I will recycle again to her husband's school so he can take paternity leave. During that time I will become retrained while back in the trenches after two years away. To Laurie and Kevin Storch, and our Area Superintendent Judy Cunningham, I extend my gratitude.

As I return to the principal role, once again, I will practice what I preach by using the strategies and processes identified throughout this book. In this way I will become a better teacher for potential administrators at Stetson University.

A final acknowledgement goes to my brother and his wife Stan and Pam, their children Morgan, Jon, and Lance Stohr; Kristen and Rick Kuykendall for their continued support and encouragement throughout this writing project.

About the Author

Leanna Stohr Isaacson is a veteran educator who has worked as a teacher in several districts, at all grade levels (including exceptional education), and as a principal in both the Northwest and the Southeast. She has studied and lived the challenges of the principalship from a rural and urban perspective inner-city and suburban schools, high diversity, and high-stakes environments.

Dr. Isaacson is a frequent presenter at national and international conferences. Most recently, her presentation topics have included the challenges and practical application of issues faced by principals and assistants who enter leadership positions for the first time. Additional topics relate to strategies for practical application of university coursework into the field of school leadership.

She received her BA and MEd from the University of Montana and, in 2004, received her PhD in interdisciplinary studies (curriculum and instruction; educational leadership) from the University of South Florida. She currently serves as a visiting assistant professor in educational leadership at Stetson University in Celebration, Florida.

She is the author of *Smart, Fast, Efficient: The New Principal's Guide to Success* (2005) by Eye on Education.

Preface

Who Should Read this Book?

- ◆ School leaders who want to stop for a few minutes, examine their real purpose, and think about the morals, ethics, and values that become the core of schools they lead. This provides the foundation upon which to build their mission, vision, values, and goals with school stakeholders.

- ◆ District or central office staff members responsible for supporting the principal of the future while directing principal training programs.

- ◆ Professors who teach courses in educational leadership preparation programs specifically classes targeting courses that focus on the Interstate School Leaders Licensure Consortium (ISLLC) Standards 1, 2, and 5.

  - Standard 1: A school administrator is an educational leader who promotes the success of all students by facilitating the development, articulation, implementation, and stewardship of a vision of learning that is shared and supported by the school community.

  - Standard 2: A school administrator is an educational leader who promotes the success of all students by advocating, nurturing, and sustaining a school culture and instructional program conducive to student learning and staff professional growth.

  - Standard 5: A school administrator is an education leader who promotes the success of all students by acting with integrity, fairness, and in an ethical manner.

This book responds to the literature that indicates educator preparation programs, including master's degree courses most often taken by aspiring principals and superintendents, offer limited training in ethical decision-making (Beck & Murphy, 1994). And yet, the way leaders understand and use ethical reasoning and decision making impacts virtually every decision they make and every action they undertake. Ensuring that leaders are prepared to make such types of decisions is key responsibility for leadership preparation programs (Edmonson & Fisher, 2006).

This book is meant to answer two questions: What is the practical application to identify and understand moral, ethical, and purposeful beliefs, when implementing the mission, vision, values, and goals for the school? What process would facilitate discussions that engage students in educational leadership classes and school leaders and their faculties, concerning these important concepts? Further discussion would include moral and ethical dilemmas that confront school administrators.

Professors and school leaders who need a summary of the concepts to serve as a visual representation can refer to the Appendix. This page contains statements that would generate further discussion. Definitions and descriptors occur for moral and ethical behavior with explanations of values, purpose, mission, vision, and goals.

Chapter Summaries

Introduction: The introduction describes the rationale behind this book. A brief review of the literature is included. The work of authors and researchers provided portions of the background used to express issues, concerns, and recommended strategies. A definition of terms gives the reader a practical summary of the concepts of morals, ethics, and values.

Chapter 1, "The Moral, Ethical, and Purposeful School Leader," describes ways to look into your own purpose. A *job purpose* identifies a subset of *life's purpose.* It examines the moral and ethical issues that surround your inner core. Once you have a clear understanding of your own purpose you are better prepared to identify the additional and foundational pieces that exist in the school community. Frequently missing from the development of an effective principal and assistant is the support needed to understand yourself and your purpose so you can identify and understand the motivation and talents of those around you.

Administrators must understand their own moral and ethical beliefs. Once leaders understand their own values, they are better prepared to take a proactive stance, placing themselves in the position of others when making decisions.

Chapter 2, "The Moral, Ethical, and Purposeful Administrative Support Group," focuses on strategies to arrive at a common belief system to build the mission, vision, values, and goals of the school through the lenses of moral and ethical leadership. In this way the school principal becomes surrounded by supporters with a shared purpose. In turn, the principals help others work toward a common goal.

Chapter 3, "Training a Purposeful Faculty Problem-Solving Team," focuses on strategies to use when a select group of master teachers become trained to facilitate problem-solving groups of other faculty members. In addition, this chapter discusses the additional roles a faculty problem-solving team can assume to support the administrator and become the flag bearers for the school mission, vision, values, and goals.

Chapter 4, "Schoolwide Purposeful Mission, Vision, and Goals: Beyond the Template," provides specific strategies to bring together an entire faculty. The chapter identifies each step the school leader takes when engaging all stakeholders as they create the mission, vision, values, and schoolwide goals through the lenses of moral, ethical, and purposeful leadership. The leader models the importance of faculty support when going beyond the often imposed standard template of improving standardized test scores. In this way everyone understands how goals are determined and why they are important. In this way all stakeholders know the direction of the school.

Chapter 5, "Purposeful Individual Goal Setting: Finding the Needs," examines goal setting based on the specific developmental level of the staff member. Goals become either individualized or in combination with others with similar needs to improve their professional skills and talents.

Chapter 6, "Differentiated Staff Development," will focus on the real world of instructional leadership when individualizing the needs of the staff. The chapter describes in detail ways to differentiate staff development. Varieties of teachers exhibit varied levels of competence from the novice to the master teacher. Particular attention is paid to challenging the master teacher.

Not all ideas or suggestions within this book fit every situation. Each of this book's topics addresses real issues in the world of the school administrator and can be adjusted according to individual needs.

Principals and assistants want to create an organization where the quality of instruction, the development of a strong professional learning community, and high-level problem solving lead to continuous improvement in leader, teacher, and student performance. Throughout this book strategies and suggestions become part of the bigger picture.

"Final Thoughts" summarizes key issues for school leaders who demonstrate moral, ethical, and purposeful leadership with their school environments.

How Is Each Chapter Organized?

1. Chapters are organized according to a sequence that fits into the individual time schedule of the school. Each chapter stands alone to help administrators pick and choose from the information most relevant to individual needs. University students would benefit by going sequentially through the book.

2. An **introduction** precedes the topic and provides the reader with background information concerning the purpose for selection of individual topics.

3. Identified topics contain the following explanations under key headings: **When Do I Begin? What Should I Do and How Should I Do It?**

4. **Short anecdotes** from principals at all levels provide insight from the real world of principals who tell their stories.

5. **Questions and Answers** expand on areas where the reader may need clarification.

6. **Survival Tips** are listed to highlight important issues that could save an administrator from unnecessary grief and perhaps avoid some school landmines.

7. The end of each chapter provides a summary to assist the reader in selecting the chapters of greatest interest.

8. **Questions for reflection** complete each chapter. These are intended to give reader-guided reflection or to generate discussions in university or principal training programs.

9. **Supporting literature** is located in the reference section of the book.

1

The Moral, Ethical, and Purposeful School Leader

Know who we are, first; then we will better understand others.

In the new millennium, the bar is raised for a school leader. As a result we are pulled in more directions than ever imagined. High-stakes testing with a carrot-and-stick approach often overshadows the need to serve the individual needs of students and teachers. Satisfying difficult parents often contradicts our understanding of the individual child's best opportunities to learn. Federal, state, and local mandates often require an autocratic approach to leadership, yet we know the best learning environment for teachers and students occurs in a democratic school culture.

As the school leader, three critical administrative and very personal themes require continuous introspection: our moral, ethical, and purposeful leadership beliefs. Understanding these provide us with an internal guidance system needed to lead in this century.

It does not matter how long we served as a school leader; 1 year or 40, when we consistently step back and regroup, rethink, and reevaluate the core of our beliefs—we reinforce the heart of our being. Our own personal belief system and leadership capabilities provide the strong sense of direction we want for ourselves and ultimately the school.

Who Are We as School Leaders?

As purposeful leaders we understand our reason for choosing the path to assist others. We recognize that by accepting a position as educational administrators we have an important role to fulfill. Teachers, students, and parents need someone who will guide them—serve them; as we prepare students for the next phase of their lives when they leave our schools; when we support and serve teachers in their quest to hone their craft.

In spite of the craziness that can surround our job, we realize the importance of our place in the world of school. We stay the course because we see value in providing leadership. Our purpose: Serve the teachers, students, and parents by modeling moral, ethical, and purposeful values.

When Do I Begin?

Daily

We need to take a few minutes every day for a mini-"think time." Also plan major "think time" to pause and reflect **if and when it becomes possible.**

Sometime during each day we need to take a few deep breaths, have a Zen moment and think about our purpose. This can happen driving back and forth to work, while in the shower, whenever. During those few minutes it is important to continually ask, "Who am I? Am I remaining true to my moral and educational ethical beliefs? What is my purpose?" Continue to analyze and define our inner self in order to better understand others.

Administrators talk to themselves (Isaacson, 2005). Parker Palmer (1998), said it best, "People who learn to talk to themselves may soon delight in the discovery that the teacher within is the sanest conversation partner they have ever had" (p. 32).

What Should I Do and How Should I Do It?

Before we check our management "to do" list, as we begin thinking about our day, first think about ourselves. Examine concepts that differentiate how and why we do what we do when leading. Reflect on our job purpose and place it at the top of our list. Do not assume that "it just happens."

As a purposeful leader, separate the defining issues about **how I am acting, and decisions I** am making as the moral, ethical, and purposeful leader. Then we will discover the commonalities and examine the interrelationship among these as the chapters unfold. This requires continuous reflection.

The Moral Leader

Moral leaders demonstrate their relationship to those they lead with terms such as: fairness, honesty, truth telling, justice, and promise keeping. A moral leader is concerned with whether the decision-making process and the impact on the school community reflects concepts of justice and equality (Ciulla, 2005). School leaders must continually make difficult decisions. Understanding our moral and ethical position on educational issues provides us with the necessary tools to make hard choices.

A moral leader demonstrates key qualities that affect decision making. After answering each question below, ask, "how do I know?"

- Do I create a democratic environment for the school personnel?
- Within the democratic model, do teachers follow my lead so they, too, create a democratic environment for their students?
- Do I lead by doing what I know is right? Do I feel it in my heart?
- Do I act to create the best possible learning environments for students and teachers?
- Do I respond proactively to school issues?
- Do I make moral decisions that ensure I "do no harm" (Starratt, 2004)?
- Do I lead from two perspectives: not only what is "right" but what is "effective?" (Sergiovanni, 1992).
- Do I make decisions based on the needs of students and teachers first, before my personal needs?
- Do I show equal respect and provide equal treatment to all members of the school community?
- Do I make every effort to create positive relationships with the school community?
- Am I a truthful person?
- Am I sincere?
- At the end of the day can I say, "I did my best to serve well?"

As a moral leader there is the need to examine the real issues placed before us, examine the data, and face the reality of the situation (Nair, 1997). For example, a frequent concern among assistants and principals occurs when the results of standardized test scores arrive.

A moral leader will:

- Analyze and report the results from multiple perspectives.
- Present information truthfully to those affected by the data.
- Report sections of the data only when we decide if this decision would not cause "harm" to any one or any group (Starratt, 2004).

- ◆ Engage the stakeholders in productive discussions.
- ◆ Differentiate among the possible solutions as the group brainstorms options.
- ◆ Make decisions primarily "through reason and judgment" (Beckner, 2004).

As a school leader our moral values may be tested as we examine key concerns that are imposed from the outside. How would we explain the moral issues in the following True Story?

True Story

High-stakes testing placed enormous pressure on our school. Our scores were not improving at the rate expected. We had a lot of low-performing students who were not as successful as they were supposed to be according to the district projections. I was told that I had the responsibility to "get those scores up." So, I didn't know what to do. I knew it wasn't what I thought was the best thing to do, but it might help get the scores raised. I eliminated science and social studies from the elementary curriculum so we could concentrate on math and reading.

—Elementary school principal

- ◆ Is it morally right to deny students a broad-based education?
- ◆ Is it morally right to make decisions that impact an entire student body without supporting evidence that it is the best thing to do?
- ◆ Is it morally right to solve a problem with a "quick-fix" solution and ignore long term ramifications?

True Story

When I received the test scores I realized that something didn't make sense. I withheld the scores until I could figured out what to do with the information. I couldn't figure out why the students as a group within the entire grade level did not do as well as in previous years. Nothing had changed regarding the demographics or curriculum.

I decided to tell the staff that the scores were inconsistent with what I knew was happening with instruction. I believed teachers were doing a good job and this was just a little set-back.

—Middle school principal

The Ethical Leader

In his book *Ethical Leadership,* Robert Starratt (2004) defines the difference between ethics and morals. "Ethics is the study of what constitutes a moral life" and "the underlying beliefs, assumption, principles, and values that support a moral way of life" (p. 5).

Ethics is also described with concepts such as integrity, loyalty, kindness, courage, generosity, and compassion. Ethical behavior occurs in relationships with others. Most often one thinks of acting ethically as common "horse sense." After all, doesn't everyone know the difference between right and wrong? In order to determine how this affects us, as school administrators, it is necessary to further examine ethical issues that surround purposeful educational leadership.

Different stories are used that illustrate decision making based on moral and ethical issues. How would we handle the situations? Were there ethical issues involved in the stories? What were they? How are they different?

Flagrant examples of immoral or unethical decisions usually make the headlines. As a leader in the education world, we are held to a higher standard of personal moral conduct. We can recall the headlines that blare, "School Assistant Principal Found Guilty of ...". As school leaders, we are expected to meet those higher standards both in and out of the school. We have heard over and over the importance of setting an example by modeling the behavior we expect of our staff.

True Story

I received a phone call on Sunday morning from the assistant principal saying, "Last night I was arrested and charged with soliciting a prostitute who turned out to be an undercover cop." This is an assistant who was with me for years. I just couldn't believe it. Sure enough, it made the headlines on the front page of the paper. The time spent on the problem was enormous. He lost his job, and I lost an assistant I thought I knew. Where were his morals?

—High school principal

Although this is an extreme example, it still happens. This assistant could try and argue that what he does on his own time is "no one's business." It does not work that way. Personal moral standards are under serious scrutiny when working in schools. The simple rule: "Don't do anything that will make headlines or embarrass our boss."

We will rely on our ethics often, not because we follow a list of our personal ethical rules that we check off once they are accomplished. Moral decisions often occur in school from an ethical perspective as we act or react to issues relating to human interactions.

At that point, we rely on our conscience when ethics is involved and we sort through the details while examining all components of problems to solve. Our own moral standards provide guidance toward ethical leadership as we ask ourselves the following:

♦ What is the worse thing that could happen if I decide to do this?
♦ What effect would this have on the staff as a whole?
♦ What effect would this have on subgroups?
♦ If the decision affects only some subgroups, which groups?
♦ Is the decision fair to all involved?
♦ Will the results positively impact our students; our teachers; our parents?
♦ Will I make this decision carefully and analytically, based on a clear understanding of the actually facts?
♦ How can I motivate my administrative support team, and the staff to put the interests of the group above their own?

"Leaders need first to be ethical and work to create an organization that has rules and policies that are consistent with ethical procedures.… They then seek to create a climate within which the employees in the work organization follow ethical principals" (Tyler, as cited in Cuilla, Price, & Murphy, 2005, p. 114).

By what standard can we judge whether or not the issue before us is one that can be described through a moral or ethical lens? The following statements may help. They are re-created and reported in Adler and Elmhorst (2005).

♦ "Treat others as we want to be treated." (This statement, essentially the Golden Rule, is re-created in many different forms in almost all cultures.)
♦ Immanuel Kant's Categorical Imperative: Could our society continue to function if everyone acted this way?"

Budgetary issues required a decision to hire only one additional staff member to support the teachers and students. The principal decided to hire a reading coach who would assist the lowest 20% of students according to the standardized tests instead of an additional drama teacher.

- "The Utilitarian Rule: Does this action do the most good for the most people over the greatest period of time?"

We received a tenured teacher from another school. Over the last two years we provided support and assistance to help the teacher improve. The teacher is unable or unwilling to meet the standards set at our school. She appears to make little attempt to follow suggestions. We completed the paperwork for two years and planned to dismiss the teacher. The teacher, anticipating her dismissal seeks a job at another school. The receiving principal calls to verify the evaluations. The principal is happy to see the teacher leave, saving him from further hassle. He gives high marks for her performance.

- "The Professional Ethic: How would this action be judged by an impartial jury of my professional peers?"

We make a bargain with the student body. If they raise their reading test scores by 3% on the standardized test we will dress up as a clown and dance on the roof of the school.

- "The *60 Minutes* Test: Would we be comfortable explaining our behavior on the famous national television show!" (Adler & Elmhorst, 2005, pp. 13-14).

When Moral and Ethical Leadership Converge

As moral and ethical leaders, we demonstrate ways to care for each other: students, staff, parents, and community members. Moral and ethical leadership converged and made the headlines as school leaders across the country guided students, parents, and staff in response **to the needs of others.** The 9/11 New York attack in 2001, the back-to-back hurricanes in Florida in 2004, and the multiple disasters of the Gulf Coast hurricanes in 2005, all rallied support from people everywhere. The dramatic plea to meet basic needs became a rallying cry to extend help.

Support for people outside the immediate school community occurred beyond the personal needs of most citizens. The disasters provided the opportunity for students to understand and participate in a real experience—responding to those who needed help. Moral, ethical, and purposeful beliefs became interconnected in the response of both children and adults.

In the problem-solving process, both moral and ethical questions often come into play. It is easier to resolve problems when the facts and options are clearly defined. For example, if the test scores of students in the middle school math class are consistently improving, the need to change the curriculum is unnecessary. The decision is easy. It is morally and ethically "right" to maintain the existing instructional strategies. Ethical issues that are clearly defined and fall into the categories that are obviously, "the right thing" do not keep us up at night.

Moral and Ethical Dilemmas

Decisions that are not all that clearly defined between right and wrong can become messy. As principals who makes moral, ethical and purposeful judgments we want to examine the issues from every angle. We understand that solutions are based on a variety of considerations: our purpose, vision; mission, circumstances, consequences, effect on others, perspectives, legal requirements, and district requirements. Decisions are often based on the conclusion that it is the "best thing to do for the greatest number."

The following provides a dilemma to solve and strategies to assist in decision making from a moral and ethical perspective:

True Story

> The math classes in the middle school have a record of improved test scores. The teachers are committed to the existing program being used. They like what they are doing.
>
> The principal receives notice from the central office that, beginning the following year the math program will change for all middle school students throughout the district. (The district wants continuity across all middle school math classes.) Now what?
>
> An ethical dilemma occurs. Why change to an unknown program when the existing program works well?

It helps to put the dilemma down on paper to help plan a strategic solution.

- ◆ Describe the problem.
- ◆ How much time do we have to come up with a solution?
- ◆ Why is the problem a dilemma? Is it a moral dilemma based upon personal or interpersonal issues?
- ◆ Is the problem an ethical dilemma? Is the issue one that will focus on what is good for certain individuals as opposed to what is good for a larger group?

- Will the solution resolve the problem in the short term, but become problematic in the long run?
- What group or groups will be most affected?
- How many teachers will that include?
- How many students?
- Is there enough money in the budget to support the mandate?
- What does the data from the school, using the existing program, show?

If we use our moral beliefs in order to make an ethical decision, what would we want to do? Do we make the decision alone, and then blame "those district office people who make us do this?" Or do we need to get a group together to work through to a solution?

Example of solutions from a moral perspective:

1. Hold the math teachers harmless at this point. (Involving the head of the department might help if we have no math expert on our administrative team.) We know that each teacher has a commitment and a strong belief that their math program works. We agree. We know the battle on our hands if we announce that the county program will be "better" and that teachers will need to learn a new program.

2. Gather the data.
   - Use existing test scores over the last two to three years.
   - Study the research about the "county required" math program.

3. Meet with the administrative team.
   - Explain the findings for the proposed math program.
   - If we are not a math education expert, then we ask someone who is, to also examine the research and provide insight.
   - Identify the difference between the programs—the one we are using and the "new" program.

4. Create a report explaining why we recommend keeping the existing program.

5. List the names of the people involved in the discussion (supervisors like to know that it was more than just us making the decision, especially when parents become part of the process).

6. Meet with the supervisor and plead the case based on our analysis of the issues.

Moral and ethical dilemmas come in a variety of forms as illustrated in the following:

True Story

> The hardest part of my job occurs when I have to tell a teacher that I am not recommending him or her for the next year's contract. Even when I have done all the things I know to do to help the teacher improve, there are times when I see that they "don't get it," and it appears as if they won't--ever.
>
> The teacher often gives me a long story about why they need the job, they need the insurance the school job offers, they need a job that fits with their child's schedule, they love the school, love their team—we have heard it all. It still does not make it any easier.
>
> Then I feel guilty, even though I know that morally and ethically, I can't let the teacher work with the students in our school if we are going to accomplish our mission.
>
> —High school principal

What are the moral and ethical issues involved in this decision?

The Purposeful Leader

Up to this point, we have examined very complex and in-depth parts of our job. We read about the importance of understanding moral and ethical leadership.

The next step is to determine our purpose. When parents, students, and teachers react to the full moon on Friday the 13th, in a torrential downpour or blizzard at dismissal time, after we've been in a two-hour lockdown, we need to refocus on our job purpose. This helps us live through crazy times, and it also defines who we really are and the essence of our being.

We will divide our job purpose into its relevant parts. Our purpose will be our personal commitment to ourselves and others. This purpose is based on our inner core beliefs and values. Then there are those beliefs and values that are part of the larger school purpose involving others for the mutual benefit of everyone. This is where the concepts of morals, ethics, and purpose start interconnecting.

When Rick Warren wrote *The Purpose Driven Life* (2002), 20 million copies were sold at first count. The speculation occurred that all over the world there were those who felt it was time to reflect on the lifestyle that surrounds the twenty-first century person. Warren's book was spiritual in nature and profound in its content. In that sense, moral beliefs combine effectively with purpose. Without any attempt to overstep the religious position, place the idea of a job purpose as a subtext for a purpose driven life.

There are times when we are so busy managing the school that all other aspects of our job seem moved from our daily "to do" list to a "wish I could" list. The importance of continuously examining our purpose is not only wise, but critical. Identifying our job purpose will allow us to keep in perspective what we are all about. It becomes an important focus as we begin our day, as noted earlier in this chapter.

The small list of people recognized for their contribution to their various fields demonstrate that purpose-driven people understand the importance of "being true to themselves." They found their "niche, their passion." They recognize a job that needs doing, and they set about doing it, often in the face of incredible obstacles. They have a crystal clear vision and purpose.

Most of us will not rise to the level of fame afforded these purpose-driven people. But we appreciate and admire their dedication, commitment, and yes—purpose.

- ◆ Martin Luther King
- ◆ Susan B. Anthony
- ◆ Louis Braille
- ◆ Mary McLeod Bethune
- ◆ Thomas Edison
- ◆ Clara Barton
- ◆ Frederick Douglass
- ◆ Chiang Kai-shek
- ◆ Cesar Chavez
- ◆ Crazy Horse
- ◆ Walt Disney
- ◆ Oprah Winfrey
- ◆ Tiger Woods
- ◆ And hundreds more

At the end of the chapter there is an opportunity to add to this list. Even though the majority of us may fall short of fame, we can lead passionate, purposeful lives.

Our Purpose Is Our Passion

School leadership is a complex profession requiring a strong sense of purpose driven by a passion for the role. Why are we passionate about our purpose? How does one describe a person with purpose? "People of purpose view themselves in the light of their potential and not of their circumstances…. Undaunted by criticism, these people of purpose set out to overcome any challenge they face" (Cheyney, 1998, p. iv).

Our Job Purpose

Robert Greenleaf (1977) described personal purpose as one's "life work or the job we were sent to do" (p. 179).

Answering the following questions may help formulate your purpose:

- ◆ Describe your personal purpose. Is it different from your job purpose? In what ways?
- ◆ Whom do you know among your colleagues that has a clear sense of their job purpose? How do you know that?
- ◆ Go back to the time when you decided to go into the field of education. Did you consider other options? What were they? Why education?
- ◆ What qualities make us people of purpose?
- ◆ What needs can you identify for teachers and students to ensure they will experience continuous improvement in their learning?
- ◆ When you maintain your deep passion and conviction that each staff member will continue to improve their strategies for instruction and assessments, what will you do to make that happen?
- ◆ How will you promote and model ideals of tolerance, compassion, and fairness (Sergiovanni, 1992). What will you do specifically?
- ◆ When you create and demonstrate a democratic process, what will that look like?
- ◆ How will you create an environment where caring for each other is part of the culture, and develop a family-style support system that nurtures diversity for the teachers, students, and parents. What will it look like?

Our Personal Mission for the School: Servant Leadership

Servant leadership is a concept that became identified in the work of Robert Greenleaf in 1970, with a mission of leadership that continues to grow. A purposeful leader can effectively use the servant leadership mindset when developing a personal mission. It is possible that statements found in our purpose will be recreated in our mission. After all, our purpose is our passion, our mission.

When creating a personal mission statement, we as school leaders, must consider the different roles we perform in life. "It requires that we understand what we hope to accomplish in life and how relationships with others inform and contribute to those accomplishments. The relationships among and between school stakeholders and how those relationships contribute to the overall purpose of schooling must be considered as the mission statement is crafted" (Fiore, 2004, p. 25).

The following guidelines identified by editor Larry Spears in *Reflections on Leadership* (1995) are based on the 10 characteristics of a servant leader that serves as the predominant model for effective leadership. A revision of those characteristics could include our personal beliefs of leadership. Some key phrases may help sort out our mission. Remember that our mission identifies how we will demonstrate to others the essence of our school. How do we demonstrate our mission to the school community?

- ♦ We listen to verbal and observe nonverbal communication.
- ♦ We hear the message of those who are talking.
- ♦ We reflect continuously on what we see, hear, and do.
- ♦ We accept each person "as they are."
- ♦ We continually examine our own behaviors in relation to others. We will act according to our moral compass.
- ♦ We evaluate the "big picture" as we determine all issues when making decisions.
- ♦ We recognize that our job is messy.
- ♦ We have the ability to relieve stress so we won't impose our anxieties on others.
- ♦ We use our powers of persuasion to guide others, not through coercion, but through rational discussions based on thoughtful analysis of the facts.
- ♦ We build consensus to drive the problem-solving process with those closest to the issue.
- ♦ We envision the future for the staff and students. We will look beyond test scores for creative ways to reach innovative goals.
- ♦ We recognize the balance needed to successfully demonstrate management and instructional leadership skills and talent.

- We examine each issue keeping the end in mind and working backward (Covey, 1991). We analyze past practices, and examine current issues.
- We also use our intuition when developing a plan leading to solving problems or making decisions.
- We commit to serve others.
- We commit to ensuring the personal and professional growth for ourselves and others.
- We encourage and involve the school community in the functions and development of the school.

As we continue to formulate our personal mission statement, the following questions may serve as "thinking points."

- When students leave our school at the end of their experience, what personal and academic achievements would they have attained?
- When students leave our school at the end of their experience, what would they have gained from teachers, both personally and academically?
- When parents leave our school at the end of their experience, what would we want them to recall about their experiences at the school?

Our Personal Vision for the School

It is one thing to think about our school vision. How will we make our commitment overt? How will a vision reflect the "what" we expect teachers and students will need to feel, know, be able to do, and act, if they are to meet our mission?

When writing a vision statement we ask, "What might this school become?"

Personal vision statements bring clarity to our purpose and mission. A clear vision provides us with the emotional strength needed to sustain us when the times are tough (Brown & Moffett, 1999).

Our Values

The values statement follows and asks clarification on *how* we intend to make the vision a reality. According to DuFour and Eaker (1998), the "values question represents the essential ABCs of school improvement because it challenges the people in the organization to identify the specific attitudes, behaviors, and commitments they must demonstrate in order to advance toward their vision" (p. 88).

When guided by our moral compass, we realize that our vision occurs when we clearly understand and demonstrate our values. James Champy (1995) identified values as the "link between what we feel and what we do" (p. 78). Values become our "non-negotiable." We will hang onto them for dear life. Values however, are not sequenced in order of importance. "One value is not as good as any other value in school" (Senge, Cambron-McCabe, Lucas, Smith, Dutton, & Kleiner, 2000, p. 278).

We demonstrate our personal values and our sense of purpose in the following examples:

- Show through actions and responses that we place our primary responsibility in helping others improve.
- In addition to celebrating teacher's hard work and dedication we will point out the positive attitudes exhibited toward reaching the school vision.
- We will demonstrate a high level of work ethic. We understand our work days are longer.
- We will focus on instruction **for the majority of the day.**
- We will remain committed to collaborative decision making with issues that affect student learning.
- We will find time to plan together.

Questions and Answers

Q: If I involve others in the decision concerning our mission and vision, then why do I have **to reflect** and think all of the other parts of moral, values, and purpose on a personal level? Won't all that come out as a group?

A: As a purposeful leader, we must remain clear and steadfast in our beliefs. We know in our heart and soul what we want to happen in our school. It is based on the research we studied, effective school practices we want to encourage, and the needs of the staff and students we analyzed. In this way we will understand if there is a disconnect between what we believe and what the existing culture demonstrates. Otherwise, we can be convinced by the vocal minority about something that is not in the best interests of our teachers and students.

A strong conviction also provides us with the grounding we need when times are tough. We can see through smoke screens, and respond logically.

Q: It sounds as if there is a lot of overlapping among things such as the difference between morals, ethics, purpose, mission, vision, and values.

A1: Each of the components identified has unique and specific characteristics. The overlap comes when a decision involves multiple pieces and it involves one or sometimes all of the parts. (See also the Introduction.)

A2: The Appendix may provide the visual that will help illustrate the components discussed.

Q: How do I keep all of these concepts straight? I could forget the language of my mission, vision, values, and goals. My moral, ethical, and purposeful leadership beliefs seem too abstract to put into writing.

A: This is the reason that we need our own time and space to think all of the components through. Write our mission and vision down, knowing they will change as our school culture changes. In the remaining chapters, it becomes essential that we know our own position and beliefs. Then, when others identify their own understanding of the concepts, we can lead them based on a mutually agreed upon direction.

 **Survival Tips**

Gray areas involving moral and ethical issues that affect decisions we must make can become very complex. This usually involves not right versus wrong but right versus right. These are not life-threatening issues, but those that often develop when dealing with people who "don't use common sense" when handling situations. We can seek advice from our trusted colleagues or supervisor. If necessary, have the rationale ready to present to those affected by the decision; remain truthful.

Do everything we can to stay out of the headlines. When morality or ethics is questioned, the difference between a "regular citizen" and a "school leader" is the size of the font in the headlines. Imagine who gets the biggest font?

Truthful leadership results in trust. It requires an administrator to reveal the information as soon as the facts are in evidence and it is a "done deal." A sure way to drive our faculty crazy: tell them every piece of information that we receive, the minute we receive it, and before we can confirm that "this is the way it has to be" only to find out later that the rules changed. This generally happens with a decree from "above" (even central office people are known to change their minds).

Write our mission, vision, values, and goals. Identify our moral, ethical, and purposeful beliefs. Put it all in short, but clear statements. Keep them visible. In the upcoming chapters, we will work with other groups to determine how each individual and group identifies the same concepts. First, work through the process alone. Keep the belief statements in writing to help maintain personal focus.

Summary

The premise of this chapter: As purposeful leaders we begin by examining the highly complex and in-depth beliefs from a personal perspective. We spend time analyzing and determining our own sense of the mission, vision, values, and goals through the lenses of moral, ethical, and purposeful leadership. In that way, we have a clear sense of our own beliefs before we engage others in a similar process.

As the leader, motivating employees becomes a direct result of the staff determining the fairness or lack thereof, and how we utilize our authority. Asking the key questions of moral leadership identified earlier in this chapter becomes key. When encouraging faculty to follow rules and policies, Cuilla, Price, and Murphy (2005) identified one way to understand what it takes to motivate others: "Employee behavior is shaped by the resources that the organization provides to support adherence to rules and policies" (p. 115). Providing a fair and equitable process to make decisions also motivates others concerning their moral attitudes and values.

The ethical leader examines issues from a variety of perspectives in order to perpetuate a high moral standard. This provides a framework from which to judge whether decisions will be the best, right, and the correct thing to do for the school community and the individuals affected by the decision. We lead in a way that is not only "right" but "effective" (Starratt, 2004).

Identifying our purpose is paramount to an administrator. We chose to lead and participate in the learning of a school community. On those tough days (and they do happen as we well know), reminding ourselves of our purpose will reaffirm the importance of our job and the role we play in the educational process of those around us. "It is up to the school leader, particularly in light of ISLLC Standard 1 (see Preface, p. xi), to lead others toward the creation of a common purpose for schooling" (Fiore, 2004, p. 25).

Establishing our personal values provides the role model for the school community. We demonstrate how students, faculty, and parents should act. This takes the form of our attitude and our behavior toward others. It shows who we are and what we believe. In the process we express our passion for our work in positive and upbeat ways. "Values are our moral navigational devices" (Champy, 1995, p. 78).

Continuous reflection becomes a critical strategy for the purposeful principal. It is a priority. We know we make time for the things that are important to us. There are no excuses for ignoring issues that require solving problems, examining our behavior under difficult or challenging circumstances, thinking of the best parts of our job, and selecting ways we can make things better.

Self-awareness and self-reflection distinguish highly effective principals from those who are "merely going through the motions." This reflection involves several mental processes including "a constant grappling with the tough issues of ethics and values in education through reflection and meditation (McEwan, 2003, pp. 158-159).

A moral and ethical leader will provide the model for the staff to follow. As a result, the school becomes one where a culture of moral, ethical, and purposeful behavior exists. The following traits are evident:

- ♦ Continuing to focus on the needs of the teachers and the students as learners.
- ♦ Treating teachers and students with consideration and support (Blase & Blase, 2003).
- ♦ Living truthfully is fundamental to a moral leader, even when we may be wrong. This "forces us to acknowledge the data and to take the important first step of recognizing reality" (Nair, 1997, p. 22).
- ♦ "Considering the well being of others is at the core of ethics" (Cook, 2005).
- ♦ Relying on ethical and moral values will not solve the problem, but gives direction and points the way (Kidder, 1995).

When we proceed through the process of understanding our moral, ethical, and purposeful beliefs, then our desire for a mission and vision for the school becomes easier to define. Sergiovanni (1992) describes this as the heart, head, and hand of leadership. We provide the road for us and the school community to travel together.

Although we strive to be the very best, we recognize that we have the same shortcomings that exist among all mortals. We will make mistakes and stay awake nights worrying whether we made the best moral or ethical decision. We will question if we are remaining true to ourselves and our purpose.

> Scholars should remind us that leadership is not a moral concept. Leaders are like the rest of us … it is only when we recognize and manage our failings that we can achieve greatness. (Kellerman, 2005, p. 13)

Making Connections

As a school leader we make ethical and moral decisions throughout every day. The continuous bombardment of competing demands on our time allows us little opportunity to think about the fundamental, yet critical issues of our core beliefs.

The responsibility is ours to collaborate with others as we determine the mission, vision, values, and goals of a school and view these foundational pieces through the lenses of moral, ethical, and purposeful leadership. The issues are too important and the consequences too great. We must understand who we are, what we stand for, and to whom are we responsible. Once our belief systems are firmly planted, then we know our purpose. Our purpose will not waver in spite of often difficult situations.

As Rebore (2001) said, "if the decisions of administrators are not prompted by their core values, their decision making will be dislocated from their genuine selves and certainly will be manipulated by circumstances and whims" (p. 47).

Application

1. Spend a few minutes reflecting and answering the following questions:
   - What are my moral standards?
   - What are my educational ethical beliefs?
   - What is my job purpose?
   - How do I demonstrate our educational value system?
   - What is my purpose in serving the school?
   - What should the school look like, feel like, and sound like?
2. A *True Story* in this chapter described a principal's decision to eliminate science and social studies from the curriculum in order to raise test scores in math and reading. With a partner, discuss the decision

you would make if test scores were not improving in reading and math regardless of the level where you work—elementary, middle, or high school. What steps would you take while maintaining your ethical and moral integrity?

3. Think of a time when you had to make a moral decision. Explain the situation and why you determined it was a moral issue.

4. Think of a time when you had to make an ethical decision. Explain the situation and why you determined it was an ethical issue.

5. Who would you include on our list of people that you view as demonstrating a strong sense of purpose? Why did you select that person?

6. What is your job purpose? A common response: to make a difference. Then, ask yourself, "What does that mean—difference for whom—in what way?"

7. Identify key values that you hold as important. Share these with your partner.

   ♦ In small groups list the values we believe are critical to demonstrate effective leadership.

   ♦ Determine the ones that appear common to the group.

   ♦ Create a common list.

   ♦ Discuss or list how a school leader would demonstrate those values.

8. What is the practical application of understanding moral, ethical, and purposeful beliefs as it applies to the school leader? For example: In applying moral principles, Sergiovanni (1992) writes that "leaders have the moral responsibility to make people feel welcome, wanted, and a part of the school with which they are affiliated" (p. 30).

9. **Review the descriptions of moral and ethical behavior throughout this chapter and determine the circumstances that could occur at a school placing the school leader in a moral and/or ethical dilemma?**

"When truth controls action, we move toward complete congruence between words and deeds … thinking and acting truthfully."
                                                                            —Gandhi

2

The Moral, Ethical, and Purposeful Administrative Support Group

Creating an administrative support group provides us with a group we trust. They follow our lead when implementing the mission, vision, values, and goals for the school through the lenses of moral, ethical, and purposeful leadership. This drives everyday interaction and long-term decision making requiring continuous reflection "about what is" and "what needs to be."

As the school organization becomes more complex, it becomes important to train an administrative support group to facilitate problem-solving and decision-making groups in order to support the school mission and vision. In this way the team speaks with a common voice. The foundational pieces that drive consensus-building processes are clear and supported among all members of the administrative support group (Elmore, 2000).

The team may consist of new members, a group that remained unchanged over the years, or a combination of both.

We facilitate focused discussions and begin asking the hard questions:

♦ "What issues require a strong ethical, moral, and purposeful team? Why not simply go about doing what needs to be done? Why should we take time to discuss things that we assume everyone practices and understands?

- How can we demonstrate our expectations for the administrative support group so they view their responsibilities as moral, ethical, and purposeful leaders?

- How can we focus a support team on the essence of the school and go the heart of what we hope could occur for all teachers and students?"

- How can we model the process and purpose of a substantive school plan with the team so that it sustains over time and generates learning among teachers and students?

- How can we utilize the administrative support group to develop teams of people who help focus the plan while aiding others in making the critical connections between the plan and their role in accomplishing it?

School Improvement Plans: Creation or Rubber Stamp?

Administrative support groups assist us in both large group and small group settings when discussions and planning occur. Throughout the chapters, the review and development of a schoolwide improvement plan becomes an example of working with large group planning. This demonstrates ways to involve everyone within a school when decisions affect all members of the school community beginning with our immediate support group.

The terms "mission," "vision," and "school improvement plan" have been around long enough that the implementation is as unique as the individual school districts and schools that apply the concepts. A school plan is intended to improve student and teacher performance.

What if the plan is not working; either in total or in parts? What if teacher and student improvement flat-lines or declines? What happened to render the plans and the implementation incongruent? Discussions with principals around the country, personal experience, and students in my educational leadership classes yield similar responses and attitudes regarding those questions.

The crunch for time and the pressure of "getting a plan together" appears to diminish the importance of having everyone in the school involved in the process of creating and implementing a substantive blueprint for improved progress for teachers and students. Ownership and understanding of the plan by members of the school community vary.

Many veteran principals describe the process of developing a school plan as something that must be done; not because of the value but because it is a district and state requirement. "We have done a plan so often by now that we can write that thing in no time;" "Innovation often flies in the face of improved standardized test scores, so we just do what we need to do and get on with it."

When questioning teachers about the last time a discussion occurred concerning the school mission and vision, answers vary: "I don't know, the vision was written when I got here;" "We talked about it during the meetings before the year began, and everyone seemed fine with it. I just don't remember what it was." Another response, "The central office tells us what the school district mission is, and we follow it; we read the vision every year, but it stays the same."

When asked, "Who on the faculty and school community was responsible for establishing a common mission, and vision?" the answers also can range from one extreme to the other, from, "The administrative team writes the plan, then the rest of the faculty hears the plan; we don't have the time to get everyone involved" to, "I don't know," or "A group of teachers writes it and we agree."

Some schools focus all of their vision and mission statements on the basis of improved test scores. The tidal wave of high-stakes testing often overshadows the needs of teachers and parents to examine the big picture of what we want for students to know and be able to do before they leave school. In-depth beliefs concerning purpose and values become overlooked. The intent of collaboration as a process in helping a school improve is lost if it becomes a fill-in-the-blank exercise framed by a central office or state-driven template. It is not uncommon to read a plan that states: "*Three percent* of the students currently at *level one* will improve to a *level two in reading* by June, based on the standardized test scores." Then the administrator merely plugs in the numbers.

Selected teachers may suggest staff development, coaching, and student remediation as solutions. However, the results of staff development as a solution without an in-depth plan for the creation, implementation, and assessment over time yields limited results (Guskey, 2000).

Another scenario could occur. The administrative team and the teachers created a process that appears to be working. Then it is put aside, filed in a notebook somewhere, and forgotten. When this happens, it is not uncommon for everyone to cruise along. Individual beliefs and strategies for school improvement can take on a "we're doing the best we can" attitude, or "we figured out what to do, now we will do it—end of story."

Without revisiting the entire course consistently, it is possible that if the tide turned ever so slowly, members of the school abandoned ship and we didn't even notice. This can happen easily as new faculty is added, during the year, or if new leaders came aboard and no one had a clear sense of where the new leaders are going. This can happen when we are busy with the hectic schedules and heavy demands on our time to keep the ship on course.

If the intent of revising the school mission and vision is simply to go through the motions, then don't waste anyone's time. If we are only rewriting the same statements as an effort to think that the school will now become better, it won't happen. This becomes an exercise that could simply replicate realigning the deck chairs on the Titanic.

A perfectly formatted document for the sake of "creating a neat and tidy 'plan' is worse than a waste of time" (Reeves, 2006, p. ix).

True Story

> I read the school improvement plan when I took over as principal of the high school. It looked good. It was clear. Then, I tried to figure out what it meant and I couldn't figure out how we could achieve the goals. So I asked some of the department chairs to tell me the mission and vision of the school and no one could even tell me what it said, let alone how we were to accomplish them. The goals were all driven by standardized test scores.
>
> —High school principal

True Story

> When my principal asked me how my instruction was supporting the school vision and plan, I didn't know what to say. I never heard that I was supposed to keep that as part of my teaching strategies. I knew the school had a plan and there is a vision statement hanging on the wall of my classroom, but I never looked at it. As a team we certainly never talked about it. I never made the connection.
>
> —Middle school teacher

How could this happen? As a principal we need support. We cannot do such a complex job alone (Reeves, 2006). If we try to accomplish every part of our job by ourselves for whatever reason, we can create a perfectly formatted document with all the parts completed as required. However, there is a major flaw in that approach. One person cannot sustain the momentum needed to effectively reach the needs of the teachers and students over time.

Overwhelmed principals often do not take the time to develop skills in others who share in the problem-solving and decision-making process. It does take time up front. The end result is worth the effort. We need to develop a strong administrative support group (Marzano, Waters, & McNulty, 2005).

Developing an Administrative Support Group

An effective team can provide us with quality assistance. They become a group who can lead others, think through issues, and ask questions. They also support the agreed upon mission, vision, values, and goals. This is the group who will reach out to other teachers to support the critical connections from the vision to the instructional application. All of this is accomplished through the lens of moral, ethical, and purposeful leadership. We then have others who will speak through one voice.

This group becomes complementary extensions of each other. The administrative team's strengths balance ours and we balance theirs. The resulting effort and support provide us with three things: (1) Everyone owns the purpose and plans; (2) Everyone shares the responsibility to become the continuous visible presence for teachers, students, and parents. The result-- administrator's time is spent in classrooms, interacting with staff, while promoting the vision, mission, values, and goals for continuous improvement for both teachers and students; and (3) All members of the administrative team posses the skills, strategies, and processes needed to work with both large and small groups in collaborative discussions concerning the mission, vision, values, and goals of the school through the prism of moral, ethical, and purposeful leadership.

When Do I Begin?

Identify time during the early part of the summer to meet with all of the administrative team; the sooner, the better. Do not rush the process.

What Should I Do and How Should I Do It?

The Process of Creating or Recreating the Administrative Support Group

The process begins when we create or regenerate an administrative support group. Whether our administrative team consists of 25 members of the group, such as in large high schools; or two, the principal and secretary, those around us provide the first line of support. This becomes more than a team; it becomes a support team for each other.

A first step could begin with an introductory letter:

To the administrative team:

During the days of _____ this summer we will meet for an in-depth look at a variety of critical issues. The following agenda provides us with a summary of the discussion points. In this way we may have time to think about ideas and suggestions we could bring to the meeting. We will explore our thoughts and beliefs, while answering important and fundamental questions concerning the following:

What are the fundamental beliefs that make us who we are in the context of moral, ethical, and purposeful leadership? What is it? What does it mean? How do we model these behaviors?

In what ways do our beliefs match the mission, vision, values, and goals for the school? How will we determine ways to serve the teachers, students, and parents of our community to ensure the highest level of success possible for everyone?

Not only will we discuss the concepts noted, we will examine and practice a decision-making model. In this way we will not only understand the foundational beliefs we demonstrate for our school community, we will find the most effective tool for problem solving and decision making.

At the completion of our time together, we will collaborate on how we will lead our school with the highest level of integrity, and assist others in creating the best possible learning environment for teachers, students, and parents.

Sincerely,
Principal _____

Treat this meeting as if it were an official board meeting of a big company.

This is a serious meeting with important foundational issues to discuss. The meeting place should reflect the important nature of our time together. Even if this is the same group of people we talked to the day before, establish a tone that signifies "today is important." The introduction to our time together sets the tone for the day.

- ♦ Arrange for refreshments and food for the day
- ♦ Organize the materials at each area with new supplies: pens, writing pads, mugs, school items with the logo; etc.
- ♦ Formal agenda

- Copies of:
  - the existing school plan including any mission, vision, values, and goals statements;
  - data from standardized test scores; even if we already examined them; and
  - school calendar that indicates instructional days (Isaacson, 2005).
- Arrange for a recorder to create minutes
- Chart paper
  - Each chart will provide topics for brainstormed ideas as each topic occurs.

As Principal—Our Personal Agenda for the Meeting Includes:

Creating substantive formal questions where the administrative support group defines their moral, ethical, and purposeful beliefs as school leaders.

- Leading the team through the same self-reflection we experienced in chapter 1. These often unspoken and assumed concepts, when articulated, provide the important basis for the heart and soul of effective leadership by each member.
- Examining each member's understanding of the school's mission, vision, values, and goals. In this way every one of our support members will perpetuate the common beliefs and philosophical foundation that guides all other discussions and activities throughout the school.
- Discussing each other's strengths and determining those who best serve the specific needs of teachers, students, and parents. Plan for the team members to spend time talking and laughing about individual personality strengths using a personality inventory of choice.
  - When responding to personality profile information, the laughter generated from acknowledging each other's idiosyncrasies creates a way to understand and identify how to work as a team and recognize individual behaviors in a light-hearted, yet, meaningful way.
- Listing the members of the team and their current responsibilities.
- Recognizing and discussing areas where each member of our administrative support group needs additional experiences and strategies.
- Discussing whether there is a match between each team member's strengths, personalities, interests, and the assigned tasks.

- Engaging in reflection of the current state of the school to determine if we need to brainstorm ideas for a "course correction" (Reeves, 2006) when meeting with the faculty problem solving team discussed in chapter three.

Assessment

- Create an efficient system to assess each of the abilities of the administrative support group as they analyze issues, solve problems, make decisions, and self-assess their own effectiveness.
- Examine and identify problem-solving models. The team determines the one that most closely fits our needs. Problem-solving strategies are assessed and evaluated for their situational effectiveness.
- Determine our administrative support group's buy-in to the mission, vision, values, and goals through the lenses of moral, ethical, and purposeful leadership through careful observation.

The Meeting

The meeting opens when we review the agenda. We set the stage with a positive tone for the meeting. Identify the importance of digging into the fundamental elements of moral, ethical, and purposeful leadership. Describe the beliefs and behaviors before discussing the mission, purpose, vision, values, and goals.

Moral Leadership Support Team

Morals

Returning to the definition by Ciulla (2005), moral leadership exemplifies itself in concepts such as justice and equality. Research findings of Tyler point out that "attitudes, values, and behaviors are strongly linked to evaluations of the procedural justice of organizational policies and practices" (Ciulla, Price, & Murphy, 2005, p. 116). In other words, as long as administrative decisions are perceived as fair, employees view the policies as "consistent with their own moral values" (p. 117). The buy-in is greater.

> **Key Words:**
> - *justice,*
> - *fairness,*
> - *equality*

In opening discussions, however, issues of morality usually begin with comments about what moral behavior is not. Lack of personal morality becomes illustrated in newspaper headlines and examples are endless. Frequently, discussions begin with stories from "other schools."

School Leader Accused of Improper Behavior Toward Students
Harassment Suit Filed Against School Leader

Principal's guiding questions:

♦ Why should we discuss issues of moral leadership among ourselves and those we lead?

♦ What does it mean and how do we know when we are demonstrating moral leadership?

♦ How can we support each other as we model moral leadership?

♦ In making decisions there are several key concepts to keep in the forefront of our behavior. What are they?

Possible answers include:

♦ We will collaborate with teachers when we need to make decisions that directly affect them; we demonstrate a democratic environment for everyone: students, staff, parents, and each other.

♦ We will model how to ask the questions that generate teacher's or community member's advice.

♦ We will make decisions based on what is the "right thing" to do, for an individual or group in our school.

♦ We will anticipate issues and concerns and become proactive. Highly complex issues should return to the team and principal to develop a response in the best interests of our teachers, students, and parents in the school community.

♦ We must make decisions based on what is best to serve the needs of others. Even though we may not like a decision based on our own personal needs.

♦ We will provide truthful answers to questions. "Honesty here is openness; giving appropriate, truthful, and timely information.… Dishonesty is the withholding or distortion of appropriate information" (Nooteboom, 2002, p. 95).

♦ We will approach issues with sincerity.

♦ We will treat everyone fairly and equally; students, staff and community members.

♦ We will respond to issues with one voice to demonstrate that our team is a support team to the principal and school as a whole.

Items are listed by the recorder on chart paper for continuous discussion and future reflection.

Ethical Leadership Support Team

Issues relating to ethics produce similar emotional reactions as those described in the discussion concerning moral leadership. Lack of ethics also generates stories that make headline news:

> Key Words:
> - *loyalty,*
> - *generosity,*
> - *courage*

> *"Embezzlement of Funds by School Principal; School Principal Vacations on School Time"; "Principal Fired for Mishandling of School's State Test Scores"; "Principal Suspends 58 Low Performing Students During Standardized Testing Days".*

The principal or assistants become the topic of conversation in the teacher's lounge without the newspaper headlines in such statements as: "We never know what is going on around here, the administrators just make snap decisions and never let us know what is happening. The administrator doesn't like me and gave me an unsatisfactory evaluation without ever talking to me about it. The administrator made me raise the grade for one of my students because of pressure from the parents. I send a disruptive student to the office and what happens? They send her right back to me with no attempt to support me with some form of disciplinary action."

Tyler reports: "Empirical research on leadership discovered that the perceived ethical character of managers has a strong influence on the degree to which employees commit to the company, follow work rules, and adhere to ethical guidelines" (in Ciulla, Price, & Murphy, 2005, p. 113). As an administrative team, it becomes essential to discuss issues of ethical behavior and ways the team will demonstrate the commitment to lead in an ethical way.

Principal's questions:

♦ What does it mean and how do we know when we are demonstrating ethical leadership?

♦ What does it look like when we demonstrate those characteristics? More specifically, how can we support each other as we model ethical leadership?

♦ In making decisions there are several key concepts to keep in the forefront of our ethical behavior. What are they?

The literature describes ethical leadership in several ways (Adler & Elmhorst, 2005).

Possible answers include:

♦ We need to treat others the way we want to be treated.

♦ We need to think what would happen if everyone at our school acted this way.

♦ We must decide if the decision would do the most good for the most people over the longest period of time.

♦ Would we want our names and the situation to appear in the headlines?

♦ We must treat adults and children with compassion and encouragement (Blase & Blase, 2003).

♦ We must examine our decisions to make sure we, "do no harm" (Starratt, 2004, p. 22).

♦ We must model our expectations regarding how teachers and students treat each other.

Purposeful Leadership Support Team

> **Key Question:**
> • Why are we here?

The next concept to discuss concerns our job purpose. This important attribute of leadership will define our passion and commitment to this organization.

The discussion could begin with our team describing the characteristics of those they read about, know, or wish they knew, who exemplify people with purpose. What is there about their behaviors and contributions that demonstrated a strong commitment and passion for their beliefs?

Principal questions:

♦ What do we believe is our purpose in our job? Why are we here? (DuFour & Eaker, 1998).

♦ What is our purpose as a member of the administrative support group?

♦ What is our leadership role?

♦ What qualities do we possess that define who we are as a member of the administrative support group?

- How will we know that the teachers are consistently creating the most effective environment for student improvement?
- How will we know if teachers are improving their craft?
- How will we demonstrate, promote, and model ideals of tolerance, compassion, and fairness (Sergiovanni, 1992)?
- What values do we instill in the adults at our school the values we seek in each other?
- What does servant leadership mean? In what ways would we demonstrate the concept of servant leadership (Greenleaf, 1997)?

Possible answers include:

- We will help create the best possible learning experiences for our teachers and students.
- As members of the administrative support group, we will consistently spread the word about our mission, vision, values, and goals for teachers and students.
- We will participate with teachers during their training sessions in order to demonstrate our desire to support them. In this way we will better understand their needs.
- We will understand each other in ways that create collaboration.
- We will facilitate and promote understanding of each other. Teachers and students need the same tools.
- We need to know how to help teachers and students who are not getting along, or when personal conflicts occur.

Charts will contain statements that identify the moral, ethical, and purposeful concepts as the discussion proceeds. The charts remain on the walls of the meeting room and provide focus and talking points when moving on to the next portion of the school plan. Through consensus building the administrative support group agrees on the foundational concepts.

The Five-Year Plan

Next, our team needs agreement on a five-year plan from the administrative perspective. Whenever appropriate, refer back to items from the charts that remain posted from earlier discussions regarding moral, ethical, and purposeful beliefs. In this way the team will make the critical connections from foundational ideals to implementation of the mission, vision, values, and goals.

The five-year period helps administrators discuss what it takes to implement consistent progress and in-depth learning over time for students and teachers. This part of the conversation becomes an "if-then" discussion using Covey's (1991) recommendation of working backward. In-depth discussions require analyzing what students and teachers need on a continuum in order to reach the five-year goals?

The process of facilitating the discussion with the administrative team continues to reinforce the tone that we are all in this together. The team identifies the current state of student and adult learning and projects high expectations for improvement within five years. Then, go back and review how to meet the targets.

We provide opportunities for each of the members of the administrative team to describe the issues that they see as important, and why. We examine the successes and analyze the problems (Marzano et al., 2005).

As principal, we create discussion points.

1. Describe our vision for the school in five years.
2. What do we know about the learning needs for our students when they enter the next level of their formal education or work force?
3. If we are preparing our students for jobs that do not exist at this time, what skills and abilities become our responsibility?
4. Do we want our school to provide the same or different opportunities for learning for our students and teachers?
5. What do we know about the competence level of our existing faculty? What should we anticipate concerning their needs over the next five years (Cotton, 2003)?
6. What is the trend of our teacher attrition rate?
7. What will it take to continually improve the school's vision, mission, values, and goals over time even when members of this team and faculty members may leave the school?
8. What are our priorities?
9. How many key issues can we logically implement on schoolwide issues without becoming overwhelmed?

Before beginning the last part of the meeting, decide the most appropriate places in the discussions to insert our personal beliefs. The timing depends on how far away from the current culture our mission and vision fall. For example, the administrative support team examined the existing data of student improvement and found that a traditional approach to student learning and teacher instruction that dominates the current culture of the school creates a flat trend line. The last two years show minimal trend in student learning in all grades. Questions to ask our support team:

- How entrenched is the culture of tradition and does that affect student progress?
- How will we approach the concern over lack of student progress and the need for change?
- What questions should we ask the faculty to begin making changes in the current mission, vision, values, and goals?

Another scenario could exist: Our school shows continuous progress. Teachers are comfortable they are "doing the right things." Our administrative support group believes they only need to concentrate their efforts on those "who have less than acceptable test scores." At this point we will refocus on the mission, vision, values, and goals.

In his book, *Good to Great,* Jim Collins (2001) states, "Good is the enemy of great. It is one of the key reasons why we have so little that become great. We don't have great schools, principally because we have good schools" (p. 1).

- If our school is good, how can we make it great? If our school is great, how can we make it fantastic?
- What strategies should we devise to challenge those who make the school good or great, to become better than before?

The Current Plan for the School

First, we want a clear understanding from all the administrative team concerning the current state of affairs within the school. Second, we want them to watch the discussion and problem-solving process we will model in order for each of them to do the same thing when meeting with the faculty problem-solving team (chapter 3), teachers, and parent groups. Begin with the plan created for the upcoming school year.

A brief review of:

- the current year's plan: mission, vision, and values;
- the whole school goals and strategies;
- the timeline for implementing each of the components; and
- the resources needed.

The Problem-Solving Process for the Administrative Team

- Given the discussion on the current mission, vision, values, and goals, describe the process we plan to use with the faculty problem-solving team and later with the entire faculty.

   An easy decision-making model for training purposes is a simplified version of the Nominal Group Technique (described in Fiore, 2004). In this model, each topic requires individual responses; similar ideas are grouped together; the statements identified as most important are placed on a chart, and later combined in a first draft document (chapter 3). If this model is not the one preferred, it does not matter. Whatever problem-solving model we choose, we will use the same one with the team.

- Role play with the administrative team each of the steps in the process.

   - Even if the mission and vision statements are generated at the central office, we use this exercise to acknowledge an agreement (assuming there is one). One step at a time, we will continue through the process until we arrive at the administrative team's mission, vision, values, and goals for the school.

- Understanding how to implement a problem-solving process becomes the purpose of this activity. We want to provide the administrative team with the tools to work with groups in problem solving, consensus building, and decision making.

   - Facilitating the process requires practice. That is the reason we rehearse with our administrative team first. All of us can discuss the key elements in the process that will generate ownership in the outcome. We can identify ways to approach each portion of generating a school plan. We can practice ways to formulate questions to small groups and individuals as they discuss issues.

Follow the same model for discussing the mission, vision, and values that we will use with the faculty problem-solving team: charting beliefs, ideas, and suggestions.

As the discussion with the administrative team continues, ask questions such as:

- What or who is standing in the way of our increasing student and teacher performance?

- As we review our school calendar, how many instructional days are lost for test practice, school events, and interrupted class time?
- We identified our five year plan, given the current state-of-the-school are we moving along? If not, why not?
- Are we all moving along according to our vision, mission, and values? If so, how do we know? If not, what is happening?
- Is there a connection between what we say we will do in our school plan and our belief system?
- Do we embed our beliefs concerning moral, ethical, and purposeful thinking for our staff and students? If so, where is it stated? How are the concepts supported by the administrative team?

During the meeting, strong operating principles and agreements reached will determine the effectiveness of the team. The discussion becomes a powerful vehicle to get at the core of each member's belief system. Through effective mediation as the school leader, we model strategies for resolution. The statements "values, or 'truths' transcend the differences that can divide groups in times of stress or conflict" (Marzano et al., 2005, p. 105). The framework provided through earlier discussion on ethical, moral, and purposeful beliefs becomes foundational to the next state of reexamining the mission, vision, values, and goals. They remain a constant point of reference.

Mission and Purpose

Key Question:
• Why are we here?

The Central Office may generate the school district's mission. Naturally, that becomes the governing mission. Each school should look at the mission statement and add parts that make this generalized statement into one that more specifically addresses the needs of our community's school.

"The focus [of the mission] is not on what the group can do, but rather why it is doing it in the first place" (DuFour & Eaker, 1998, p. 58). The "mission establishes an organization's purpose" (p. 62).

Key questions:

- Does our mission statement continue to reflect our beliefs for all members of the school community?
- How do we know?

- Does the mission statement reach out to the future of our students and teachers?
- In what ways do we consistently reinforce the mission to the teachers, students, and parents?

Vision

Key Question:
- *Where do we want to go in the future?*

"A vision instills an organization with a sense of direction" (DuFour & Eaker, 1998, p. 62). When developing a vision, clarity becomes critical. "By definition, vision contemplates the future, and the future inevitably involves uncertainty, change, and fear … leaders can use vision to build trust" (Reeves, 2006).

For example, as the school leader, we believe that the school should move from the existing traditional approach for all students to a vision that students and teachers should solve problems and make decisions based on critical, creative, and conceptual thinking. We realize that this is a big leap from the current culture of the school.

Specific questions provide a clear sense of the vision for each of the team members.

Key questions:

- "Does our vision statement continue to reflect our mission?
- How do we know?
- In what ways do we continue to reinforce the current vision of the school?
- We already discussed our vision for our school in five years. Is there a difference in expectations for our students five years from now and our plan for the next year?
- In what ways?
- If we want areas of instruction to improve for our teachers, how can we support them in that effort? For example, if we want areas of instruction to include teachers using strategies for students to make decisions and solve problems through critical, creative, and conceptual thinking, what will it take to make that happen?
- What kind of resistance could we expect from our teachers if we began identifying a more progressive approach for curriculum, instruction, and assessment?
- What are some strategies for changing our vision from one of traditional approaches to more progressive ones?

Values

According to DuFour and Eaker (1998), "the values question challenges people within the organization to identify the specific attitudes, behaviors, and commitments they must demonstrate in order to advance toward their vision."

As the school leader we already identified our personal ethics, morals, and values. Once we begin working with our administrative support group it becomes necessary to discuss key questions to reaffirm the meaning of each of the beliefs that accompany the mission and vision. The key question: What are our values?

Key Question:
- *How will we grow a staff that commits to our goals, takes care of each other, and continues to improve?*

"A team cannot share values if the values have not been shared with the team" (Maxwell, 2001, p. 183).

Key questions in addition to those we, as the leader, identified in chapter 1, are:

- ♦ Are we remaining true to our values? Do our values transfer from our administrative team, to the teachers, to the students, to the parents?
- ♦ The greatest deterrent to school improvement comes when faculty members exhibit competing values. Conflict resolution requires a clear sense of our values
  - What ones do we ignore?
  - What values do we reinforce?
  - How do we treat each other?
- ♦ How do we know when we demonstrate our core values?
- ♦ What do we see as valued in our school both with our colleagues, students, and parents?

Goals

Goals determine measurable steps the school community will take to achieve our vision and mission. They provide both short-term and long-term opportunities to provide continuous improvement or make adjustments in the learning experiences for both students and adults.

Questions and discussions around the concept of goals identified up to this point by us as leaders, and our support group, determine schoolwide issues compared to goals needed for individuals, departments, or teams.

- Achieving goals that directly affect all members of the school community with a whole school focus often occur with such behaviors as: attendance; discipline; bullying; or homework or those that begin the process of changing instructional approaches toward more progressive strategies for all content areas.

- Goals that would include the grade level or team such as: implementing a grade-level interdisciplinary conceptual unit of study; adopting a new grade-level strategy for the teaching of writing; or implementing a new program in a grade level or department.

- Individual goals that help a teacher improve their current skills and talents in working with students.

  Discussion questions could include:

  - Do our goals reflect ways to improve the learning of our teachers and students?

  - Do the goals for departments or grade levels reflect a progressive approach to teacher and student learning?

  - How will we develop open dialogue between each of us and each staff member to make sure we are meeting their needs?

Getting the entire administrative support group to reach consensus on key components that drive the school community becomes critical since our team interacts with staff and community members on a consistent basis. They spread the current message and we want it to be the same vision, mission, and values. If the same team has been together for two years or more, are there built-in assumptions about what each believes? Often, groups have worked together long enough that they think they know what everyone else believes. But, do they? This is the time to find out.

True Story

> I became principal of a school where the previous administrator was an institution. She had been there for years and everyone "did their own thing." The faculty all followed the one textbook for each subject, line and verse. I was so far on the other end of the continuum from where they were it wasn't funny. I kept thinking, "Where do I even begin?"
>
> As far as I was concerned I needed to fix everything—now. My colleagues were right with their advice, "Take one thing at a time."
>
> When I met with the administrative team for the first time, I listened very carefully to their beliefs. I found the one part of the entire plan that I could live with. I started with the most compatible thing and embedded a small part of my beliefs into the one place I could. I knew I would need a lot of patience.
>
> —Elementary principal

Questions and Answers

Q: This seems like a lot of time to spend on talking about such abstract concepts. Morals and ethics are what they are. Why talk about it?

A: Discussions about moral, ethical, and purposeful leadership provide a solid base for problem solving when conversations get bogged down with more trivial issues. Once we reach common agreement among our own team members, all of the other dimensions of school leadership fall into place. Each understands the foundation for decision making.

Q: It is easier to just delegate tasks to the assistants based on the things that need accomplishing. Why spend so much time on training a team to work with others?

A1: Delegating tasks occurs logically for management assignments, such as, overseeing facilities, taking care of discipline, working with the noninstructional staff members, or scheduling custodial tasks. But, the fundamental concepts that provide the foundation for school improvement where all members of the community participate and understand the core values of the school requires help from a well-trained, knowledgeable team. This takes time. That is why the summer schedule should include time to work on developing the team.

A2: In January, schedule two days of time when the administrative team meets and discusses the areas described. Each member must be available. Any one person left out of the loop will require individualized training. Everyone needs to build the school's foundation together.

Q: When I work with the administrative team during the summer, it seems like I am talking out of both sides of my mouth. On one side I want collaboration from everyone on the mission, vision, and values. Then, I tell the team what I believe. That seems like it would stop the administrative groups from assuming any "buy-in."

A: The talent of a purposeful principal comes in the ability to facilitate and support a group in "finding their own way" through the process of problem solving and arriving at their own decisions. During the process, if we see the resolution to the problem is significantly different from our own, we embed our own questions into the process.

- What can I do to make this work for all of us?
- What concern us that we haven't talked about before?

Survival Tips

- *Remain upbeat, enthusiastic, and motivated.* Revisiting the school plan should sound as if this were the first time we ever created one. An attitude that portrays the mission, vision, values, and goals as unimportant conveys the same attitude to the staff. The total message on moving onward and upward becomes lost. As a purposeful principal we recognize the significance of continuously reinvigorating our school for each person, regardless of the time it takes.

- *Create a different environment for the problem-solving meeting.* If we revisit the school plan every year, then create another way to approach our past presentations.

  - Perhaps we can find another site; a conference room at another location—hotel, restaurant, or club house, for the problem-solving team meeting.

  - Locate some door prizes; create a "professional" environment with a few new bells and whistles when the entire staff comes together.

  - If we want to create the feeling that we are going to move upward and onward then provide an atmosphere that demonstrates the importance of the "good to great" school plan.

- *Don't rush the process.* We need as much time as it takes to complete the problem-solving process effectively. This is the reason we start early in the year, so we are not rushed.

- *Training our administrative support group* sets the stage for each of the members to facilitate future problem-solving groups.

- *Provide minitraining sessions in the same improvement planning processes for assistants hired after the year begins.* New administrative assistants (and teachers) hired after the school year begins face the same problems of adapting to their new culture. Take time to walk them through the same issues, processes, and discussions we provided our team during the summer. Otherwise, the new members have no idea how to support us and their colleagues.

- *Each member of the administrative support group receives clearly identified statements that define the mission, vision, values, and goals through the lenses of moral, ethical, and purposeful leadership.* When developing the same concepts with the schoolwide faculty, statements will become modified. This provides each member of the administrative support group with a draft to use when facilitating their small groups in chapter 3. (Note: the team should not impose their statements on the small group; rather, these statements contain the language with which to focus.)

Summary

Ethical, moral, and purposeful leadership defines the heart and soul of our team and everyone who makes the school remarkable. These beliefs are clearly discussed and articulated with our administrative support group.

Once the business of creating an improvement plan begins, then problem solving becomes a work in progress. During this chapter we learned about the process of working with an administrative support group who identified their beliefs. They in turn lead others through problem-solving and decision-making processes.

Reeves (2006), describes this as "messy" leadership. "The practice of reviewing data, making midcourse corrections, and focusing decision making on the greatest points of leverage—is superior to 'neat' leadership in which planning, processes, and procedures take precedence over achievement.... The keys are monitoring, evaluation, values, beliefs, and implementation" (p. xi).

When a principal faces a complex issue to resolve for the first time, he or she often creates a problem-solving model that begins with personal self-reflection (chapter 1), and identifies a method to bring consensus and understanding of the mission, vision, values, and goals with the administrative support group.

As the leader, our beliefs are logical, sound, and based on solid evidence. Haynes (1998) describes a system of ethical decision making when the administrator and administrative support group ask three sets of questions:

♦ "What are the consequences, both short and long term, for me and others, and do the benefits of any possible action outweigh the harmful effects?

♦ Are all the agents in this situation being consistent with their own past action and beliefs? That is, are they acting according to an ethical principle/ethical principles that they would be willing to apply in any other similar situation?

♦ Do they care about other people in this situation as persons with feelings like themselves?" (pp. 28-29).

We are passionate about what is best for teachers and students. Repeating our beliefs to the administrative team on a frequent basis is a good thing.

Perhaps something happened in the school that caused us to rethink old beliefs. Whenever we have a change of heart about our belief system, regardless how small the shift, the administrative team needs to know.

The Moral, Ethical, and Purposeful Connection

Ethics, morals, and purposeful leadership require an in-depth understanding and consistent demonstration of these concepts. As leaders, our self-reflection provides the foundation on which to guide the discussion with our support team. The short version of the concepts follows:

- **Ethics:** The fundamental demonstration of ethics occurs when the leaders consider the well-being of others before themselves.

- **Morals:** Leadership that responds to "do good, ... by exploring how to use institutional resources to improve the good that schools are supposed to be providing—namely, quality learning for all kids" (Starratt, 2004, p. 39).

- **Mission/ Purpose:** Our purpose "becomes the standard we use to evaluate which activities are essential and which aren't ... our purpose determines how we base decisions, allocate our time, and use our resources" (Warren, 2002, p. 31).

When a school, grade level, or department see themselves as good, determine if good is good enough, or is great, great enough? Can a good school become a great school?

Course corrections become part of the process. They are done carefully, with involvement from those directly affected, and with clear evidence that a change, however small, is necessary.

Making Connections

- Discuss the reasons why we should invest the amount of time indicated in order to understand the moral, ethical, and purposeful beliefs of the administrative support team.

- What is meant by, "it is all about the process?"

- Provide examples of a moral dilemma and what decisions would we make?

- For example, an influential and aggressive parent demands we override the teacher's decision to change the "only 'B' my child ever received," to an "A". What are other examples?

♦ Provide examples of an ethical dilemma and what decision we would make.

- For example, we change the letter grade without consulting the teacher, or we require the teacher to change the grade.

♦ What are other examples?

♦ Provide examples when an administrator either lost sight of the purpose and vision; or fragmented the purpose and vision originally established by the groups. What would we do as a member of the team?

- For example, the original purpose and vision for the school identified the key focus for the teachers and students: *Teachers and students will solve problems through critical, creative, and conceptual thinking.* The administrator concentrates all his or her efforts on emphasizing the importance of winning the state championship football game.

- What are other examples?

Creating an administrative support group provides a key group that speaks of the same mission, vision, values, and goals. Creating a problem-solving model that each understands and will implement for whatever situation requires a group decision. In chapter 3 the team takes their understanding of the foundational pieces to build the school, a decision-making model to use, and engages in a rehearsal with a faculty support team.

One knows a leader by his or her effects on followers. "Indeed, leadership and followership are *yin* and *yang*, mutually defining their important roles in improved learning for all students and adults" (Solomon, 2005, p. 37).

> *In order to be a leader a man must have followers.*
> *And to have followers, a man must have their confidence.*
> *Hence, the supreme quality for a leader*
> *is unquestionably integrity.*
> *Without it, no real success is possible,*
> *No matter whether it is on a section gang,*
> *a football field, in an army, or in an office.*
> *If a man's associates find him guilty of being phony,*
> *If they find that he lacks forthright integrity, he will fail*

His teachings and actions must square with each other.
The first great need, therefore,
is integrity and high purpose.

—Dwight D. Eisenhower

3

Training a Purposeful Faculty Problem-Solving Team

When conscientious school leaders try to do it all, they sacrifice time with students and teachers, the very groups they want to support. "No single leader possesses the knowledge, skills, and talent to lead an organization" (Reeves, 2006, p. 28).

The principal and administrative support group will now train a group of staff members who clearly understand the mission, vision, values, and goals of the school. They serve as an outreach to their colleagues, students, and parents.

Assumptions exist that faculty members automatically know how to lead groups to resolve issues and make decisions in a thoughtful, productive way. In reality, this isn't always true. Specific training in problem solving, along with the accompanying discussions, offers strategies, tools, and resources for a select group of staff members to assist others.

The more people involved in the process of solving problems and making decisions, the more focused the school purpose and goals. The faculty problem-solving team requires individuals who demonstrate natural leadership and a commitment to the school mission and purpose, vision, values, and goals through the lenses of moral, ethical and purposeful leadership. They know our beliefs, as the school leader, and the importance of reinforcing those beliefs throughout their interaction with the staff.

Throughout the year problems and decisions require solutions involving different groups of faculty, both in numbers and in purpose. Large issues, such as schoolwide plans, or specific issues that involve the school as a whole require an entire faculty's involvement. Concerns such as individual student progress or instructional strategies unique to a content area become more easily resolved among small groups of instructional teachers.

This chapter will provide specific dialogue that a school leader may choose when explaining the concepts. It will also concentrate on developing a faculty problem-solving team who could serve in a variety of capacities:

- ♦ They become a liaison between their colleagues and the administrative support group.

- ♦ When decision making involves the entire school, each member knows how to facilitate consensus building when large groups of school members gather together. Each will facilitate the discussion with a manageable small group.

- ♦ When decision making is unique to a smaller number, such as grade level or department, these leaders implement strategies for resolution.

- ♦ Issues and concerns become more efficiently resolved when identified leaders understand a process for bringing resolution and provide the necessary follow-up.

- ♦ They understand the importance of focusing on schoolwide goals. In discussions, this group knows the language of school improvement.

- ♦ They will refer back to the terms that drive the plan: mission, vision, values, and goals. They understand the connection from the plan to moral, ethical, and purposeful leadership.

- ♦ When the administrative team wants to discuss "what if" ideas, this group provides wise insight into the issues.

Richard Elmore (2000) describes utilizing trusted members of teams to help lead an organization as *distributed leadership*. The faculty problem-solving team is smaller in number and lends itself to substantive discussions. The problem-solving team will provide insight into the current attitudes and behavior of the staff as a whole (at least based on their perception. They are good barometers). This group provides preliminary insight into issues that would guide the schoolwide discussion on the mission or purpose, vision, values, and goals.

When Do I Begin?

The sooner in the year we establish and train a faculty support team the better. The team will provide the leadership to help us, the school leader, and our support team. Training will require a day out of the classroom. In this way the team can focus on the tasks at hand.

What Should I Do and How Should I Do It?

Create a Faculty Problem-Solving Team

Identify a group that we believe will meet defined criteria and methodically analyze school issues. When faculty members are asked to "volunteer" for another "committee," either the rookie is designated or the faculty member who drew the short straw becomes the chosen one.

- ◆ This group is either appointed by us, as the school leader, or the group is selected by members of the faculty. Publicized criteria helps faculty understand who and why the group is selected and reduces the possibility of criticism for the choice of the members.

- ◆ Possible criteria could include the following:
  - Teachers with three or more years experience in the school because they understand the history behind previous practices and policies.
  - New teachers who demonstrate interest in leadership experiences.
  - A representative from each area or department.
    - guidance
    - media specialist
    - technology specialist
    - exceptional education
    - second language learners
    - art, music, physical education

- ◆ The representatives selected or identified would demonstrate the following characteristics and behaviors:
  - thoughtful;
  - clear about the big picture of a school;
  - innovative;
  - well-informed about current educational practices;
  - trusted by the faculty;
  - wise;

- works well with others; and
- any additional criteria, based on our needs as the leader.

These are the members of the staff that will spread the vision among other school members in a positive way. Yet, this is a vocal group who might be brutally frank and honest and still remain objective and insightful.

Organizing the Faculty Problem-Solving Team Meeting

The administrative support group can organize the first meeting for the faculty problem solving team by completing the following tasks:

- ◆ Oversee the selection of the team members;
- ◆ Organize the group;
- ◆ Send out invitations and an agenda;
- ◆ Ensure substitutes to cover classrooms;
- ◆ Contact the individuals for verification of attendance;
- ◆ Make sure all departments or grade levels have a representative (don't forget media and technology specialists, exceptional education, guidance, and second language learner teachers);
- ◆ Arrange for someone to record the key points;
- ◆ Arrange the facility, provide an inviting environment, arrange for food and beverages, including delivery and clean-up;
- ◆ Display posters of the district mission and vision;
- ◆ Display posters with the current school mission and vision; and
- ◆ Provide sticky notes, chart paper, pens, writing paper, tape or tacks for displaying ideas.

True Story

As a new assistant principal I was looking forward to the experience of leading a team of teachers during a planning session. The group would begin the preliminary work on the school's strategic plan. I thought everyone was participating and giving good ideas. Then, the principal started going in and out of the meeting. I found out later that she didn't have an emergency.

As soon as the principal appeared to lose interest, so did the rest of the team. The quality of our work was based on the principal's presence. I was really disappointed in the end result. None of us ended up feeling the principal cared about what we were trying to accomplish.

—Middle school principal

Problem-Solving Team Training

Once the group is selected, an invitation to each member of the selected team will identify the important task assigned to the group. The following may provide an idea of how to frame a personalized letter.

To the faculty or staff representative

Mr. Jones:

Bill, we need your help. It is time to revisit our vision, mission, values, and schoolwide goals statements. Your insight, ability to work well with others, and your understanding of the workings of the school as a whole will aid in the development of our school plan for next year.

As a preliminary step, and in order to help facilitate the process when we work with the entire faculty, I am asking us to become part of a Problem-Solving Team. A substitute will cover your class for the day we meet.

During that time I will give us and the rest of the team an overview of how we will facilitate the development of a schoolwide plan. This will give me an opportunity to explain the role us would play in working with small groups. Your help will be invaluable.

We will meet on _____ in the _____.
                        (date)   (place)

Please bring the attached documents at that time:

♦ Current mission, purpose, and vision statements for the district and school.

♦ Summary of the existing data:
  • Last year's testing information
  • Demographic changes
  • Population numbers; total school, individual grade levels, or departments

♦ New programs added to the student's options, or programs taken away for some reason.
  • Progress of students who participated in the "new program."

♦ Comparison of student performance over the last three years.

♦ Issues that emerged during the administrative support group meeting during the summer.

♦ Any other documentation in the form of data that will add important information into the decision making process:

- student attendance
- student discipline, broken down by any pattern of school rule violations
- such as bully behavior, fighting.
- graduation rates
- tardiness

(•Lists will include items unique to concerns and needs at individual schools.)

I look forward to seeing us. Let me thank us ahead of time for taking time out from your busy schedule to help in this very important process.

Gratefully,
Principal _____

Problem-Solving Team Meeting

Introduction by the School Leader

The following statements could provide the introductory discussion points. We might say something like this:

"In a few days we will have the entire faculty meet to develop (or re-examine) our school plan for the year. I need your help to facilitate smaller break-out groups. We need everyone on the faculty and staff to participate.

We know the state and district guidelines for improving our standardized test scores. Our job is to expand the template and make the school plan one that we all agree on, and we all understand.

Your ideas will also become part of the group dynamics. You will serve in both roles. Today is a rehearsal in order to identify extraneous issues and determine the focal points when the schoolwide faculty meets. We will role play the strategies we will use when everyone on the staff convenes.

The greatest challenge we will face when working with the groups is to engage each person to the extent that each one feels ownership in the process and the outcome. Throughout our discussion we will talk about ensuring everyone has equal opportunity to express their opinions, not only in our group today, but in the schoolwide problem-solving meeting."

The simulation below explains the leader's strategy for training a team to assist when a schoolwide plan is required. This process involves demonstrating how a problem-solving team facilitates small groups in a large school.

The Logistics

An easel and chart paper will stand by each table group. In this way, when the group agrees on their final ideas, suggestions, or descriptions, us as a group leader will record the information on the charts. You will collect all the charts at the completion of the time together. Members of the team will combine and synthesize the statements for later distribution.

- ♦ Each topic requires an individual chart.
  - Mission/purpose
  - Morals
  - Ethics
  - Vision
  - Schoolwide goals

Defining the Task

As the leader we could say, "As members of the problem-solving team we will be assigned a small group of faculty members to assist them as we create a schoolwide plan. We will work through the entire process. In this way, when your groups engage in dialogue, you will have the background, tools, and strategies to facilitate a productive outcome when the entire faculty meets. Your leadership will help keep the group focused and engaged in the process.

The goal: involve everyone in the process of defining, describing, and understanding the purpose and direction of our school. When the meeting concludes, each faculty member should own the plan.

Our school plan expands the district-level mandate for improvement. We will develop goals with the schoolwide faculty that meet the district expectations. We will then examine our own data and together determine the most effective method of achieving the goals for our school.

We will discuss our moral and ethical beliefs and their connection to our values. This leads us to a discussion concerning our mission and purpose, followed by our vision and schoolwide goals. Small groups and individuals will determine separate goals at another time. Each foundational portion of what makes our school effective requires taking one topic at a time. In this way we can ensure that everyone understands what drives our decision making."

Today we will identify the same topics that will be presented to the faculty. The statements prepared today, through simulation, will be for your eyes only. It will provide us with discussion points with your assigned group, since we already understand the process.

One question may need clarification. What is the difference between morals and ethics? For purposes of discussion, when meeting with your groups it helps to identify the various terms used to described both concepts.

Ethics becomes demonstrated when adhering to professional and societal values. Ethics determines our moral behavior. Moral behavior comes from our personal and cultural experiences.

Our purpose is not to debate the individual terms used to describe morals and ethics, recognizing that different authors use different descriptors. Rather, the commonly identified terms in the literature provide a reference point for discussion. This is a process to identify morals, ethics, and values as important components of how we lead the school. The question: How do we demonstrate that we will act in moral, ethical, and purposeful ways while maintaining the integrity of our values?

We will review the data documents during the time when we discuss goal setting. That will come later in the planning process.

The following decision-making model is easy to implement with large groups:

♦ **Step 1:** Provide guiding questions to the group pertaining to the concept. Follow with a discussion of the questions.

♦ **Step 2:** Role play the discussion with the faculty team that could occur when the schoolwide staff meets.

♦ **Step 3**: Write ideas:
  • One idea each on a sticky note, and
  • Place each idea in the center of the table.

♦ **Step 4:** Combine redundant statements.

♦ **Step 5:** Write single statements from the combined notes.

♦ **Step 6:** Determine if the statements meet identified criteria: For example, are the mission/purpose, vision, and goals measurable?

Moral Behavior

The leader may say, "As educators we are held to a higher standard of moral and ethical behavior. Yet, we rarely discuss what it means. Issues of morals and ethics are more than a list given to us at the beginning of the school year and found in our handbooks.

Key Words:
- *justice,*
- *fairness,*
- *equality*

Step 1: Guided Questions:

◆ *From where do we get our moral beliefs?*

Answers could include: from our values that we received growing up, our culture, parental expectations, self-imposed expectations, knowing right from wrong.

◆ *When describing moral behavior, what words do you think of?*

◆ *What behaviors come to mind?*

◆ *What do we mean when we say that we act in moral ways?*

A framed sentence will help maintain the focus:

◆ *We demonstrate moral beliefs for our students, colleagues, and parents when we_____."*

Possible answers from the faculty team (then later during the schoolwide group's meeting in chapter 5) could include:

• Consistently do the right thing.
• Put the needs of the school, team, or classroom above my personal agenda.
• Treat each person with equal regard for their dignity and fair play (Sergiovanni, 1992).
• Demonstrate the belief that all of us are part of an interdependent organization; we all need each other.
• Discuss and resolve issues honestly and with regard to the feelings of others.
• Consider the effect of my behavior on others.

Upon completing the discussion, and identified steps in the process, written statements will reflect the general consensus of the group.

Continue steps 2-6 found on the previous pages.

When statements of morals are agreed on, place them on the chart.

Ethical Behavior

A discussion of ethical behavior could begin by providing each person with guidelines for ethical behavior written by both national organizations and state boards of education. If the faculty received a brochure or list of ethical behaviors at the beginning of the year, the statements provide points of reference.

Discuss how ethics are demonstrated in the context of the existing school culture. The following words are a few examples. Solicit a discussion on the behaviors associated by describing the application of each word. These may also help us with the discussion with the group.

> **Key Words:**
> - *loyalty,*
> - *generosity,*
> - *courage*

Step 1: Guided Questions:

♦ *From where do we get our ethical behavior?*

♦ *When describing educational ethics, what words do you think of?*

♦ *What behaviors come to mind?*

♦ *What do we mean when we say we will act in ethical ways?*

The following words are a few examples to help facilitate discussions:

- virtue
- worthiness
- principled
- integrity
- authentic

♦ *We demonstrate ethical beliefs for our students, colleagues, and parents when we _____.*

Possible answers could include:

- Stop and think about the decisions I plan to make and possible consequences that could result.
- Treat all others with compassion and encouragement (Blase & Blase, 2003).
- Follow the rules mandated, whether I agree with them or not.

- Do "everything possible to serve the learning, developmental, and social needs of students as persons" (Sergiovanni, 1992).
- Take action, in spite of opposition, when acting in the best interests of the students.
- Remain honest and straight forward in actions and discussions.

Continue steps 2-6.

When a statement of ethics is agreed on, place it on the chart.

Values

"Moral and ethical beliefs lead to discussions of values. The additional emphasis on establishing a values component for the school reaches into the core of serving the needs of all members of the school community. Values demonstrate the behaviors, attitudes, and buy-in, that members of the school community: parents, teachers, and students agree to uphold." (DuFour & Eaker, 1998)

> *Key Question:*
> *▪ How will we grow a staff that commits to our goals, takes care of each other, and continues to improve?*

The school leader continues: "The agreement of values is often assumed or implied within a school culture. Identifying and discussing the school community value, places this important concept out on the table. In this way a common agreement occurs as us put that understanding in writing."

The problem-solving team is a good place to discuss the values issues and the importance of understanding the focus for the school and teams. "Just as personal values influence and guide an individual's behavior, organizational values influence and guide the team's behavior.... Shared values define the team" (Maxwell, 2001, p. 179).

The problem-solving team becomes the voice for identified values with other members of the school community. Continue the process. The group identifies the values they hold as teachers, not only to the students and parents but to each other.

Step 1: Guided Questions:

♦ *From where do we get our values?*

♦ *What behaviors come to mind?*

♦ *When describing educational values what words do you think of?"*

The following framed sentence may start the discussion.

♦ *"We demonstrate our values when we"*_____

Possible answers could include:

- Commit to personal growth within the organization in such ways as mentoring and coaching colleagues.
  - To this end Maxwell (2001) describes the importance of us, as leaders, also making a commitment to mentor others, and provide continuous support for faculty improvement.

    "to grow any organization is to grow the people in that organization" (p. 183).

- Value the contribution each member makes to the organization.
- Commit to continuous pursuit of personal academic growth to better serve the students.
- Collaborate.
- Recognize and promote the common goals.
- Trust in each other.
- Respect our differences and provide learning experiences that support the differences in learning styles.
- Recognize and provide for individual needs of staff and students.
- Support and encourage other leaders to emerge.
- Act honestly
- Act with fairness
- Maintain our integrity
- Act with authenticity and humility
- Teach problem solving through critical, creative, and conceptual thinking.
- Monitor the results of ever challenging strategies for learning and understanding ourselves and our students.

Continue steps 2-6 found on previous pages.

When statements of values are agreed on place it on the chart.

Throughout the discussion team members will recognize the overlapping descriptions. This is the opportunity to engage the team in a discussion concerning the relationships that exists among the beliefs. Our values, moral, ethical, and purposeful beliefs become the foundation for creating our mission, purpose, and goals.

Recreating the Mission and Purpose

The school leader continues, "We are now going to recreate our mission and purpose statement.

The mission and purpose provides the sonar that explores deep into the inner core of what school is all about; not a generic view, but a clear understanding by all the stakeholders regarding why the school exists. DuFour and Eaker (1998) add an additional component: "with the willingness to accept the responsibility to achieve that purpose" (p. 61).

Teachers read the existing mission and purpose statements that the school uses. "A mission and purpose are often seen as describing the same end. The mission becomes the 'why' the school family gets things done and for whom. Vision and values drive the mission and define the purpose. Vision statements will drive the goals.

Step 1. Guiding Questions to the Table Groups (if the group is large enough or to the group as a whole)

The school leader continues, "A mission or purpose creates the steps to reach the vision. It provides the targets. 'A mission statement tells what the school is all about' (Fleck, 2005, p. 5) or 'why do we exist?'" (Dufour & Eaker, 1998, p. 58).

"Our mission—What is our purpose?"

Does our current mission and purpose statement define "why" we get things done and for whom?"

Step 2. Role play the discussion with the faculty problem solving team

In the discussion with the groups keep the conversation focused.

♦ Improving teacher and student performance becomes the overarching purpose.

- Think about our mission as our purpose.
- What is the point of what we do?
- Can we measure our mission or purpose in a substantive way?"
- Since we have the district mission and purpose, in what ways can we expand that mission to include our own school-wide mission and purpose?"

Continue with steps 2-6 found on previous pages.

Since this is a small group, role play how the statements are checked against criteria. The leader asks: "Does the mission statement meet the following criteria:

- Is it short enough to remember, but substantive enough to have a clear sense of the end result?
- Is it focused, understandable, and therefore doable?
- Does it clearly state where the organization 'wants to go and how to help it get there?'" (Dubrin, 2004, p. 422).

For purposes of the rehearsal, write the final mission statement on chart paper.

Recreating the Vision

"We will now create or recreate a vision statement." The leader states, "The vision is meant to drive our mission or purpose. Martin Luther King had a dream. His speech demonstrates the effect that a passionate leader can have in describing in a clear, understandable way, a powerful purpose, and a clear vision, wrapped up together.

Or, we can dance around the substance and focus on keeping people happy such as in Rodgers and Hammerstein's lyrics and music in the show South Pacific to explain a dream:

Happy talk, keep talking happy talk,
Talk about things you'd like to do,
You gotta have a dream, if us don't have a dream,
How you gonna have a dream come true?

It makes a cute bumper sticker, and translates well into a graphic. But does it contain the substance that we can translate into action? The words hopes and dreams are not illusive. It requires definitive ways to achieve them.

Our vision changes as our school needs change. It changes as the future for all of us changes. The school moves progressively toward the desired end and requires revisiting consistently.

Step 1: Guiding Questions by the School Leader

We need to ask ourselves the following questions:

- *"Does the vision reflect not just the general consensus, but the best thinking?"* (Barth, 2001).

- Does the vision *"provide the essential bridge between the current reality of the school and what it hopes to become in the future?'* (DuFour & Eaker, 1998).

- *Does our existing vision adequately state how we plan to improve our teacher and student performance?*

- *Does our vision describe what we are trying to do?*

- *How will we make the vision a reality?*

- *What are the specific attitudes, behaviors, and commitment necessary to advance toward our vision?*

"A vision represents the hopes and dreams for students, teachers, and parents to learn in the best environment possible. It describes the future; where we want to go. It is a powerful statement. Yet, a vision is fluid. It will change as the needs require" (p. 88).

In the discussion with the group, keep the conversation focused on the positive outcomes. The problem-solving team needs to understand the issues they may confront. They will keep teachers from getting sidetracked with the problems.

The school leader guides the initial questions; ultimately the members of the faculty team will keep the focus on topic. This rehearsal provides valuable insight into the issues that may occur when the schoolwide faculty meets.

Continue steps 3-6 of the decision making model found on previous pages.

For purposes of the rehearsal, write the vision statements on chart paper.

At the completion of this portion of the meeting with the faculty problem-solving team we describe the next part of the process. The faculty team does not need to develop the completed written document at this time. The process, not the product, becomes the purpose for the faculty problem-solving team training.

- The faculty team will understand that it is too time consuming to create a final group of statements when they work with the schoolwide faculty.
- The statements created during this exercise may not be the ones the faculty determines.
- As the team they will reconvene after the schoolwide meeting to synthesize the agreed-on statements and develop a draft.

Identifying Potential Schoolwide Goals

We proceed with a different format when presenting schoolwide goals because the concepts are not the same. Now is the time when the faculty problem-solving team and the administrative support group review the documents they received prior to the meeting. This time the conversation and decisions are data driven.

Two issues determine how to proceed: time and number of faculty involved in schoolwide goals. Either way, the administrative group and the faculty problem solving teams will collaborate on the best way to present goal setting to the schoolwide faculty when, and to whom.

Presentation of the Data

When meeting with the schoolwide faculty, and later with the parents, the following data discussion provides the opportunity to focus on issues that affect the performance of students, and ultimately the faculty. At this point the faculty problem-solving team reviews the data and draws preliminary conclusions. Identified goals become the result of examining data.

What does the data show? During the summer the administrative group drew conclusions from the data. We synthesized the information and will now provide the relevant and readable charts and graphs from which to draw conclusions from the problem-solving team.

- Utilize the documents that we provided each team member.

- Provide the team members with our initial interpretation of the data. This saves time and helps focus the process.
  - Compare student performance over the last three years in all grade levels, departments, or teams.
  - Identify issues that emerged during the administrative support group meeting during the summer.
- Discuss any conclusions the faculty team reached.

Guided Questions

Discuss the following question: *"Based on the data, what schoolwide goals will provide a substantive way to reach the vision we created?"*
Role play the discussion with the problem-solving team.

"When working with the school-wide faculty groups, we will facilitate the discussion by asking questions such as: 'What data suggests we need a school-wide goal?'

- As we work with small groups, what goal could we expect may come from the discussion?
- Would this goal affect each member of the student and faculty body, or would it affect only some?
- Is the goal measurable?
- Is the goal something that will produce short term results?
- Is the goal something that supports the mission, vision, or values statements?
- Is this a goal we can accomplish?"

Goal setting discussion should rest on the issues that directly involve every student and teacher, and which ones are teachers or team specific. Further guided questions might include:
Examine the data and determine which areas on the standardized test, the grade level, or department, where student progress appears lower than expected. For example,

- Our math scores for our eighth graders remained unchanged.
  - Is this a schoolwide problem? (If elementary, the answer is yes; middle school and high school would become grade level, or teacher specific.)

- How do we want to present this information, and to whom?

Examine behavioral data such as attendance or bullying. In this way the team sorts out the issues that become schoolwide and those that are specific to individual students.

- ◆ "If lack of student attendance is an identified area of concern, determine if it is a schoolwide problem, or based on the same group of students, during the same class or time of day.

  - If only specific students are involved, to whom should we address the problem?
  - Do we want to present the problem to the school-wide faculty? Why, or why not?

- ◆ We included character education as part of every student's program last year, yet our rate of reported bullying incidences did not change. We now have reason to suspect that identified cases of bullying appear to be internet related.

  - Is this a schoolwide problem?
  - In examining the data we determined that it is still the same group of students reported. How should we approach the problem?

All of us in the administrative support group and the faculty team analyzed the data. In this way, we can eliminate pieces of data presented to the schoolwide faculty that do not involve the entire school. Narrow the field to the potential goals that include the entire school. That allows an efficient use of time, and it gets to the heart of the school's beliefs.

During the conclusion of our time with the faculty problem-solving team, we will ensure that each member is comfortable with both the process and the issues that will come before the schoolwide faculty. Each member must have the personal tools and knowledge to facilitate small groups. Ideally, each teacher will know the groups assigned so they will be prepared to work with the various personalities that exist in his or her group.

Both the faculty team, and later our administrative support group, determines the landmines—the controversial issues and the naysayers. Based upon the discussion and interaction with the team, we know the staff and how best to configure the groupings when the entire faculty meets. The members of the faculty problem solving team are now well prepared. They will serve as our voice when groups meet. As the leader, we want to be sure the faculty and staff speaks in a collective voice.

Parent Involvement

Every school creates a system to involve parents based on the school culture. Determine how and when we will receive parent input into the process. Our faculty problem-solving team knows what we hope to accomplish during the year. However, parents need involvement in the process. How will we receive information and ideas from the parents? When in the process will parents provide ideas? What process will we develop to include parent suggestions and expectations? The decision may include:

♦ Parent survey
♦ School Advisory Council of Parents

As school leader we could work with the chair of our advisory council and determine the approach.

Questions and Answers

Q: There are naysayers on the staff, and no matter what we want to do they will try to undermine both the process and the intent of our schoolwide faculty meeting.

A1: Place our strongest assistants, ourselves, or the most credible member of the problem-solving team with each group where this may be a problem. We may not end up convincing them of the value of the meeting, but at least we have someone facilitating the process who will maintain the focus. Hopefully, they will begin to understand what the school as a whole is trying to accomplish.

A1: Individuals who disagree with the process usually fuss the most about "those meetings." Yet, they are the ones who are quick to point out they don't know what is going on. Tell them they can't have it both ways. If they want to know what is going on, they need to be present to find out and become a part of the solution.

Q: How often does the faculty problem-solving team membership change?

A: We selected a core group whom we trust. As other leaders emerge and demonstrate their commitment to our beliefs, then we could add them to the team. Membership may change due to the natural attrition when faculty members leave the school for whatever reasons. A core group should remain on the team at all times.

Q: This seems like an extra step in the process of creating a school plan that is time consuming. Why take this extra step?

A1: Principals often rely on a group of trusted faculty members to help solve school issues. However, they are rarely trained in the specifics of working with small groups, resolving issues, understanding the core of the school beliefs, and supporting our goals. The group needs quality time with us so their role as problem solvers becomes clearly defined. Using them as facilitators during the schoolwide planning meeting is only one example of their value.

A2: When bringing large groups together for the one-time session to create a school plan, a process is needed to break into small group units with a trained facilitator in order to involve everyone.

 **Survival Tips**

♦ Avoid the use of voting to select members of a problem-solving team. Identify tight criteria to determine those who would make the most effective decisions and provide the school leader with the most support.

♦ *Stay with the team throughout the entire process.* As soon as we remove ourselves from the group and their tasks the message is clear—the team's role is not important. If we are not present, it is possible that the outcome becomes completely different from what we expected.

♦ *Remain upbeat, enthusiastic, and motivated.* Revisiting the school plan should sound as if this was the first time we ever created one. An attitude that portrays the mission, vision, values, and goals as important, conveys the same attitude to the staff.

♦ *Don't rush the process.* We need as much time as it takes to complete the problem-solving process effectively. Rich and productive dialogue takes time.

♦ *The more organized, the more efficient, the more productive the process.*

♦ *Include the problem-solving team's meeting dates in the school calendar as part of the overall scheduling for the year, then everyone involved schedules around that time.* They recognize their participation is an expectation because we need them to help make important decisions that could directly affect them and their students.

♦ *Create a different environment for the problem-solving meeting.* Since we revisit the school plan every year, create a different way to approach past presentations.

  • Perhaps we can find another site; a conference room at another location—hotel, restaurant, etcetera, for the problem-solving team meeting.

♦ *Celebrate the work of the faculty problem-solving team.* Groups that give of their time to help make the school a better place for students and adults require recognition. The faculty problem-solving team could receive some form of appreciation; restaurant certificates; golf shirts with their names on them; preferred parking places; or just an old-fashioned, hand-written letter of thanks from us, the school leader.

Summary

Ethical, moral, and purposeful leadership define the heart and soul of everyone who makes the school what it is. These beliefs are clearly discussed and articulated in a variety of ways.

During this chapter we learned about the process of training a core group to work with other faculty members in substantive and informative ways. Media specialists, technology specialists, and guidance staff also make significant contributions to the team. Administrators and faculty rely on their expertise to provide the needed support to the staff. They understand how to access data both from a district and state database for standardized test scores. They come in contact with every faculty member, student, and most parents. They often see the big picture from a global perspective.

A problem-solving team serves in a variety of roles for us, our administrative team, and the faculty as a whole. They become the flag bearers for the school mission, vision, values, and goals through the lenses of moral, ethical, and purposeful leadership.

"The only constant is that no one remains consistently at the apex; that position is reserved for the ideas, values, and commitments at the heart of the followers" (Sergiovanni, 1992, p. 71). Our job as school leaders requires we maintain the focus for all of the players, relinquishing the chair when others present compelling ideas to examine. As the school leader we let the spotlight shine on others as frequently as possible.

As an administrative team we can not be everywhere all the time. That is why we train another group of key faculty members. We provide them with the tools to discuss, arrive at consensus, engage in meaningful dialogue, and keep the focus.

Making Connections

Abstract concepts such as moral, ethical, and purposeful leadership fall on deaf ears unless groups within the faculty understand the meaning and how those concepts translate back in to their practical world. Identifying a key team, spending time discussing the terms and what they mean that translates back to the classroom, and placing the team in facilitative roles when faculty members need guidance, become a powerful strategy.

The problem-solving team learns the application piece of the concepts to understand their personal purpose when interacting with students and adults. When colleagues make decisions that affect others, a member of the team can help assist them as they think through the moral, ethical, and purposeful ramifications. They have the language to express their beliefs and the understanding to help others make the critical connections from the words to the actions. They serve as our other voice.

The faculty problem-solving team requires our attention. The training session becomes only one example of the role each member assumes.

Application

+ Describe how to utilize faculty members that were trained in a problem-solving process and understand the mission, vision, values, and goals for the school.

+ Discuss the advantages and disadvantages of selecting one group who is trained to assist their grade level, team, or department members in strategies to solve problems while maintaining the integrity of the established goals.

+ What would we recommend to a team if they wanted to expand the number of goals they believe the rest of the faculty could achieve? For example, what if the focus was on reading across the curriculum or higher-order conceptual thinking for all students. A couple of members on the problem-solving team want to add additional goals from other departments. How would we handle that? (Remember, this is just a rehearsal. The schoolwide faculty did not meet yet.)

+ What strategies would we use if we discover a member of the problem-solving team does not demonstrate a compatible belief system? For example, as the school leader, we believe that all teachers should instruct students in problem solving and decision making through higher-order critical, creative, and conceptual thinking. One of the team members believes that students will never learn to write if they can not diagram sentences every day. "Those kids need drill, drill, and drill."

♦ Is there a difference between ethical values and moral values? What are they? **Is it the terms that matter or the understanding what the demonstration of ethical and moral values looks like at the school? Explain. (See also the Introduction, chapter 1, and the Appendix.)**

♦ As a school leader, what key points would we want the faculty problem-solving team to understand about their role in supporting us and the school?

♦ As the school leader, to what degree would we explain the dilemma facing the school leader when moral and ethical beliefs oppose each other?

"What I do you cannot do; but what you do, I cannot do. The needs are great, and none of us, including me, ever do great things. But we can all do small things, with great love, and together we can do something wonderful."
—Mother Teresa in en.thinkexist.com/quotes/
mother_teresa_of_calcultta/

4

Schoolwide Purposeful Mission, Vision, and Goals: Beyond the Template

This chapter uses the school plan to illustrate how to implement strategies when the entire school faculty becomes involved in a problem-solving, decision-making process. In this way, everyone participates and understands the underlying issues surrounding decisions regarding the direction for school improvement.

Schoolwide goals provide the focus and compass to support each teacher and student in improving their strategies for learning. Members of the administrative support group and the faculty problem-solving team facilitate table groups in bringing consensus. We create mission, vision, and values statements through a discussion of ethical, moral, and purposeful behaviors. This provides all faculty members with tools to make decisions and solve problems utilizing the process, statements, and concepts.

Involving everyone on the faculty in the initial discussion and planning provides insight into moving the school beyond the template. Going beyond the fill-in-the-blank scripts the state or local district requires becomes one step in the process.

The school leader moderates the process for schoolwide planning. When this part of the process concludes and the draft of the school plan is written, everyone on the faculty will know where the school is going, why, and for whom. Every person will know the mission, vision, values, and schoolwide goals. This chapter will provide strategies and additional insight into the process of involving all members of the school community as they commit to the schoolwide goals to improve student learning.

If this is the first time the faculty comes together to plan, it takes about three to four hours to complete the process. The school leader decides when it is best to bring the groups together. Whether during the days allocated before school begins, or three sessions after school starts in the fall, everyone on the faculty participates.

Schoolwide Goal Setting Meeting

Role of the School Leader

- Place the date, time, and purpose for the faculty planning meeting well in advance on the school calendar.
- Announce early our expectation that everyone will attend due to the importance of their contributions to the plan.
- Plan for a professional-looking meeting such as described in chapters 2 and 3. Prepare to moderate the meeting. We facilitated the meeting with the faculty support group. They know what to expect. The entire staff discussion looks slightly different as described throughout this chapter.
- Anticipate the timing for the meeting. There is a lot to cover and time is always short. If it looks as if the discussions and conclusions last beyond the expected time, don't rush the process just to finish. Continue the meeting at another time.
- Provide each person with a copy of the Code of Ethics provided by the district or state department.
- Prepare overheads or a PowerPoint for the following framed sentences:

Mission and Purpose:
- Why are we here? What purpose do we serve for our students and for each other?

Moral Beliefs:
- We demonstrate moral beliefs for our students, colleagues, and parents when we …

Ethical Beliefs:
- We demonstrate ethical beliefs for our students, colleagues, and parents when we …

Vision (that we can measure):
- What do we hope to become?

Values:
- We demonstrate our values when we …

Schoolwide goals (that we can measure):
- How do we hope to get there?

♦ Prepare handouts for the faculty
  - A clear, concise, set of data; easy to read and interpret.
  - Disaggregated data to present those issues that are schoolwide

Role of the Administrative Team

♦ Gather and organize the pertinent data. During the faculty problem-solving team meeting, data that provided little insight into student or teacher progress becomes eliminated. Instead, it is the role of this team to consolidate the pertinent information in order to create a clear focus for teachers. The data should be clear; it must be easy to read and interpret for the facilitators as well as the faculty.

♦ Provide each member of the problem-solving team with detailed notes to help them clarify any confusion among the terms for
  - morals
  - ethics
  - mission/ purpose
  - vision
  - values
  - schoolwide goals

(See also the Appendix.)

- Assist facilitators as they guide the discussion for these abstract concepts.
- Create groupings of faculty and the facilitator.
- Display name tags and tables assigned to help put mixed personalities together.
- Grouping of the staff is flexible. The goals are schoolwide and not based on individual grade levels or departments; not every seventh grade team member needs to sit together.
- Provide sticky notes, chart paper, and pens.

The Problem-Solving Team's Role

One member of the problem-solving team will participate within each group of 7-10 faculty members seated at a table. The opportunity for groups to discuss a common question and arrive at a general consensus becomes an important part of the process. Guiding questions become the opportunity for everyone to "have their say."

- It is the job of the problem-solving team members to keep the table groups focused.
- Provide the opportunity for all staff to talk among themselves and clarify their own thinking on the subject.
- Determine the most important issues that need focus, and create the collaborative dynamics needed for all stakeholders.
- With the problem-solving group, identify the topmost achievable schoolwide goals.
- Each of the members of the group becomes familiar with the concept, issues, and language that the faculty will discuss. If needed they will help clarify the terms.
- Record information clearly enough that it will synthesize easily at the completion of the meeting.

Schoolwide Planning Meeting

Preliminary Information to the Faculty

Prior to the staff meeting, provide teachers with an agenda of the proposed discussion with instructions to talk among themselves before the next staff meeting. Some teams will elect to meet ahead of time and discuss the issues so they can get their thoughts together. The faculty problem-solving team represents all the groups within the school. In that way, when the invitation arrives, individual faculty members will contact their team representative for any preliminary questions. This is the time that the faculty problem-solving team member begins to spread the "good news" about the planning process. The notice could read:

To all faculty members:

During our faculty meeting we will be discussing key questions and we need your help. We will review our current mission and vision statements. They may need revision as we discuss values and goals as well as our ethical and moral beliefs. We will determine if they reflect what we want for our students and for you as teachers. When we meet in the _____ on _____ at _____. The following questions may help we focus on the task:

- What can we do to improve the performance of our students?
- What can we do to help you, as faculty, strengthen and improve existing practices?
- Do our mission, vision, and values statements show we are providing better opportunities for learning than before for our students and faculty? If not, what should we add or change?
- Are we providing better opportunities for student learning than we have done to this point? If not, what more should we do?

We need our best thinking as we revisit these important issues. We look forward to working together as we collaborate to make our school better than ever.

Snacks and beverages will be provided at our meeting on _____ in room _____.

Sincerely,
Principal _____

Goal Setting With an Entire Staff

During this meeting all members of the staff contribute to the discussion; this includes food service personnel, custodial workers, clerical staff, and teaching assistants.

Many of the faculty will complain about doing an activity that may in the past have been an exercise in futility because many teachers experienced the act of "doing" goals. They may complain if this becomes "another meeting."

♦ Provide food, snacks, and beverages.
♦ Explain the expectation that everyone helps create a plan with goals that will guide the entire school.
♦ Individual's plans to meet the goals occurs later (chapter 6).
♦ Explain the role of the members of the faculty problem solving team.
♦ Use humor and enthusiasm.

All faculty members participate. Unless everyone is part of the entire process, they can always say, "I don't know what's going on." We could assign regularly scheduled staff meetings to accomplish this important goal setting task.

Special recognition belongs to the problem-solving team. The faculty needs to know who they are and their role in the meeting.

The steps used in our faculty problem-solving training session are the same ones to follow during the schoolwide faculty meetings. We will modify our approach based on the number of staff. The process goes quickly when a facilitator assists small groups.

Part I of the meeting: Mission, vision, values through the lenses of moral ethical and purposeful beliefs.

For purposes of clarity, suggestions for a presentation by the school leader follow.

Introduction

Introduce problem-solving team members as trained facilitators.

The principal begins, "Our meeting today will occur in (one-three parts; depending on our time). The first part identifies the fundamental beliefs that guide us. Who are we? What is our purpose here? How do those beliefs drive our values in the way we work with our students, our parents, and each other? In making decisions today, who is the focus? Our personal needs, the needs of our students, or the needs of our school as a whole? These questions will be asked as we define our moral, ethical, and purposeful beliefs.

As we work in groups, the facilitator will assist in combining your ideas and common beliefs. After our planning session we will provide a document that details your comments so our belief system is clear.

The second part of the meeting (or next meeting) will review the most relevant data from a variety of assessment sources: standardized testing; authentic assessment; teacher documentation, etc. From the data we will determine the most important goals that all of us at our school will support.

For purposes of our time together we will narrow the goals that affect all of the faculty and students.

The third part of the meeting (or next meeting) we will review all of your statements and make sure they say what we mean. The final revision will be sent to you through e-mail or hard copy.

As soon as the schoolwide goals are clear, our individual commitment to reaching those goals will follow. We will create a process for that to occur soon after this meeting.

The first part of our time today we will discuss three critical and important concepts: moral, ethical, and purposeful beliefs. We will then identify our values.

One staff member at your table is a member of the faculty problem-solving team. They completed this discussion as part of their training as facilitators who will work with you throughout the process. Their job is to keep the discussion and activity focused so our time together is concentrated on this important part of improving our school.

Let me start with purpose and mission:

Although the school district defines a mission that we must support, we have a mission at our school as well. It is our purpose.

- Take a few seconds to think about our purpose and our mission for our school, with our students, and faculty.
- For each idea, place the sentence or phrase on the sticky note in front of you.
- Discuss the ideas that are the same, put similar ideas on top of each other.
- Find the top three; agree that they represent the group's beliefs.
- The facilitator will write the top three on the chart paper.
- If anyone has an idea that they think was not given proper consideration, it should occur on the chart as well (written in a way that identifies it as a single issue).

Place the mission and purpose frame on a visual.

—*Why are we here? What purpose do we serve our students and each other?*

Time: 10 minutes

Note: A few key terms below are used as a point of reference and consistency on the concepts of morals and ethics. Different groups may determine more effective descriptors, based on individual school communities. Use whatever terms are clearly and consistently understood yet demonstrates the concept. It is the process of discussion that becomes the focus.

Next, we will identify our moral beliefs.

Key Words:
- *justice,*
- *fairness,*
- *equality*

The next consideration concerns issues surrounding our beliefs about moral behavior. What is it? How would we describe it? And what ideas could we write to explain how we demonstrate our moral behavior for our students and each other?

The facilitator avoids discussions on immoral behavior. The headlines in the paper take care of that. Instead, what does moral behavior look like at our school?

(Repeat the same process as above)

Place the moral beliefs frame on a visual

—We demonstrate moral beliefs for our students, colleagues, and parents when we…

Time: 10 minutes

Now we will identify our ethical beliefs.

Key Words:
- *loyalty,*
- *generosity,*
- *courage*

Each of you received a copy of the state and national standards for ethical behavior. Although, once again, we know by the headlines in the paper what unethical behavior looks like. What does ethical behavior mean for our school?

(Repeat the same process as above)

Place the ethical beliefs frame on a visual

—We demonstrate ethical beliefs for our students, colleagues, and parents when we …

Time: 10 minutes

Total time: approximately 30-40 minutes

During the next part of our time together we will examine our mission, vision, values, and schoolwide goals.

"We will now examine the mission statement provided by the school district."

(Place the mission statement on a visual)

Does the district mission state what we believe is the mission of our school as well? Of course, the district statement provides the guideline. Is there anything we want to add that makes the mission specific to our school?"

Usually, the mission statements from the district level are global enough to cover most schools. This is a good time to remind everyone what it states. The district mission may stand on its own and may not need a school extension.

"We will now reexamine our current vision statement" (If there is no vision statement for the school, this is the time to create one. Place the vision statement on a visual).

"When identifying a vision, we need to answer the main question: 'What do we hope to become?' However, the decisions we make need certain criteria in order for us to decide what we believe."

"Our vision statement will drive our goals." (If the district developed a vision statement, then it should become a part of the information handed out at the beginning of the meeting.) *"If we read the district's vision* (if there is one) *and we need to support this vision, what additional statements can we make for our school?"*

As we think about our vision keep in mind some criteria:

(Place the following items on a visual)

1. Is it doable, given our resources and culture?
2. Will students be better off than they were before?
3. Is success in meeting the vision measurable?
4. Is the vision easy to remember and restate to others?
5. Does the vision affect everyone or just a few?

6. Does the vision reflect the latest in best practices?

7. The vision must be measurable. It is not enough to say we want to become a world class school, for example. How would we measure that?"

(Repeat the same process as before)

Place the vision question on a visual

Vision (that we can measure):

—*What do we hope to become?*

Time: 10 minutes

"The next area to discuss relates to our values. Values become a critical component when identifying what we are all about. Moral and ethical beliefs create the foundation that describes our values. John Maxwell, a well-known author, describes the importance of understanding our values in this way. 'Just as personal values influence and guide an individual's behavior, organizational values influence and guide team's behavior … shared values define the team.'"

Statements that define our values relates to the way we treat our students, our parents, and each other. One of the more difficult parts of being a principal is trying to resolve conflicts that occur between members of the staff. If we understand how we define our values, perhaps we will recall the statements made today. Hopefully, they will serve as a reminder about how we value each other.

In addition to the value we place on each other as professionals, colleagues, and often friends, there are other things we value at our school. This gives us the opportunity to define what we believe.

(Repeat the same process)

Place the values frame on a visual:

—*We demonstrate our values when we …*

Time: 10 minutes

At the conclusion of this set of information gathering, the charts are collected. Select someone or find a volunteer to consolidate the information into concise statements that reflect each of the areas. The end result: the faculty will receive clear statements prior to developing schoolwide goals.

Schoolwide Goals

Presentation of the data leading to the development of schoolwide goals could occur in a variety of ways, depending on the time available and the size of the faculty. Faculties of 30 or fewer can become more involved in the actual analysis of the data for the entire school. Faculties of over 75 require a more direct approach with the data.

We, the administrative team, and the faculty problem-solving team studied the data enough to know the target areas where schoolwide improvement is necessary.

When faculty members look at data, they only want to know how it affects them and their students. Provide teachers with the most important information.

There were two specific areas that we want to draw attention to for schoolwide discussion. For example, our teams concluded that if students were provided more opportunities to solve problems and make decisions through creative, critical, and conceptual thinking, they would not only improve their test scores, but improve instructional strategies. Although it appears that some students continue to make progress on their reading scores, the rate of improvement is much slower than expected.

The other area of concern is the higher than district average absentee rate.

Walking a Tight Rope

When the administrative group and the faculty problem-solving team agrees on the area of concentration for the school, how do we sell that to everyone else? It depends.

- ◆ If the data determines that we must make significant changes in the existing culture of the school, provide the information at this meeting, but do not draw any conclusions.
  - State the facts as the data shows and let everyone know that it will require a plan. We will look into the best way to involve as many people as possible in the solution.
  - Chapters 5 and 6 describe methods for individuals and small groups of teachers to begin working on a change strategy.

- If the district-level office requires something new, then that require-ment becomes nonnegotiable and becomes a statement of fact. The information is followed by the leader acknowledging that the imple-mentation of the district-office mandate will be presented to those teachers directly affected.

- If the area to improve is one discussed in earlier meetings or among faculty groups before, then it becomes an easier sell. The background is already laid for further discussion. The data supports that the issue identified previously still appears as an area to investigate and the faculty sees the performance scores.

Assume that teachers discussed the problems associated with students underperforming in reading, both on standardized and authentic assess-ment. Other teachers verified that when students fall below a specific reading level, they become unable to compete with more advanced students in every content area. Since this discussion occurs consistently among all teachers, it is possible that most everyone realizes the problem affects every classroom. Teachers want more information about how to assist with reading in class-rooms that traditionally do not focus on "the teaching of reading."

Morally, this is the right thing to happen. Teachers want the best things for their students, even if it may mean more work on their part or a change in their instructional strategies. Our response, "We will bring together a group to figure out the best approach since every faculty member can play a part in helping identify how best to solve the problem. We will meet with each of you to determine ideas on how to meet the goal." (See also chapter 5.)

For example, teachers are willing to identify reading across the curricu-lum as a schoolwide goal. Details will be worked out later. For those grumbling at their table, "I don't want that as a goal. It is not my problem." The faculty facilitator takes note that this person needs more handholding. This is not the forum for debate.

In reality, each level of schooling approaches schoolwide goals in a differ-ent way. At the elementary level, everyone concentrates on the content areas; it is the focus from one year to the next. For an entire school to agree on read-ing across the curriculum as an area of concentration would not provide a blip on the radar. However, in high school the issues are more content area specific. Particularly in large high schools, it would be almost impossible for everyone on the faculty to agree on one single area for concentration.

As a result, data drives decisions; however, those decisions in the form of school improvement plans become individualized. If the math scores do not meet expectations then the development of plans to increase student perfor-mance is decided among teams and small groups who teach in departments where mathematical understanding occurs. If the schoolwide goal, however, is reading across the curriculum, individual goals described in the next chapter could address reading in mathematics or other content areas.

Another example: Our administrative team analyzed the data and drew on our experiences in observing classroom instruction. Two issues surfaced: (1) we analyzed subtests in critical thinking, analysis, and inferential reasoning on the standardized tests and concluded that little growth occurred among some of our best students. We reasoned that if the best students' gains are slow, what must happen to the lower level students? (2) Through observations during the previous year, we saw limited questioning and discussion that provided students the opportunity to engage in higher-order thinking. As a result, instruction did not include critical, creative, or conceptual thinking. Students did not make connections around the "big ideas."

The schoolwide faculty identified reading across the curriculum as a goal; that is a more familiar concept. If the concept of conceptual thinking or instructing students to make critical connections across the content has not been mentioned before, strategies for implementation require a methodical plan.

Debrief With the Problem-Solving and Administrative Teams

After the mission or purpose, vision, values, and schoolwide goals are written, there is a need to meet with the problem-solving team to debrief. (This could occur in a short meeting.) The key question: Was there anyone in the group that we felt was "just occupying a seat"? Do we know why?

- Share any suggestions about what it would take to bring this person on board?
- Ask the group about the positive things and the negative things that occurred.
- Take notes so that the next time we engage in this activity we will avoid any problems that occurred.
- Create a draft of the identified beliefs and schoolwide goals
- Edit the agreed-on statements: Ethics; morals; mission and purpose; values and schoolwide goals. Does everyone on this team agree that the statements are clear?
- Make any changes
- Post statements along with the original draft. In this way, the problem-solving team, and later the faculty, will see where the changes occurred during editing.

As the school leader, we will provide time for the faculty and parents to respond to the identified belief statements and make changes if needed.

- The administrative team will assemble all the documentation; parent and faculty.
- Meet again with the faculty problem-solving team (after school is enough time).
- Meet with the parent group and review the information.
- Assign or ask for volunteers to create a display of the faculty and parent's work: a large poster for the main hallway; brochure; signs for each teacher's room; a Web site display; and a report to our supervisor. Mission, vision, values, and goals beliefs are powerful methods of communication.
- Finalize and publish the calendar of dates for follow-up meetings with committees, groups, or the problem-solving team. Assign members of the administrative team to review the calendar with the affected faculty members or parent groups for final feedback.
- Send the final calendar of meeting dates out to the school community.

Questions and Answers

Q: Why go through all this process when the entire school plan only tells how many percentage points we will raise the standardized test scores?

A1: If we are lucky, there is a connection between low scores for some groups and curriculum, instruction, and assessment at the school.

A2: A school plan should evolve from the needs of our teachers and students. Since all needs for students generally focus on learning, then learning what, and for whom becomes central to our plan. A fill-in-the-blank-plan may, in the long run, not address the needs of everyone in our school. Now what? Create another plan that does. Follow the data.

Q: Why should I start the process of a school plan so early in the year? Our district doesn't let us begin until spring.

A: If everyone needs to become involved, so that the stakeholders are a part of the process, we need time. Look at our calendar and plot out the times we will need. Remember the importance of our personal involvement in order to demonstrate our commitment. Start early in the year.

Q: As an administrator, what if I have a great idea but I can't get it off the ground with the rest of the staff? How do I handle that?

A: Unless it is some "off-the-wall" idea, try snooping around to see if there is history with the idea. Usually, a veteran teacher whom we trust can shed some light on the problem. We may be able to try a different approach at a later time.

Q: I'm afraid that teachers will rebel if they have to meet and participate in a seemingly lengthy process.

A: This is when we demonstrate our talents as a great communicator. People need to see the importance of their involvement. Teachers can't have it both ways: they won't understand what is going on, without being a part of the process of figuring it out.

Q: What happens if some people's ideas are not used in the final product, or they seem to stand alone?

A: Identify them on a separate chart paper. Do not forget about them, because the person with the idea will not forget. Assign someone on the administrative team to follow up and see if the idea can be used in another way. A subcommittee could address the idea if everyone agrees it is important. Otherwise, place it in a visible area so that the idea is still acknowledged as a valid one.

Q: When I work with the administrative team during the summer, I want collaboration from everyone on the mission, vision, and values. Then, I turn around and tell the team what I believe. That seems like it would stop the administrative team from any ownership.

A1: The talent of a purposeful principal comes in the ability to facilitate and support a group in "finding their own way" through the process of problem solving and arriving at their own decisions. During the process, if we see the resolution to the problem is significantly different from our own, we embed our own questions into the process.

A2: If we don't let those closest to as (the administrative team) know what we believe, they will not know how to support us. Assistant principals have the responsibility to follow our lead. If their ideas and beliefs appear radically different from ours it becomes important to work together and determine discrepancies.

Q: When should we include the parent input into the process?

A: The leadership and problem-solving teams will determine the most efficient and effective process to receive parent input. Often the school district requires a specific survey. Individual schools may have a questionnaire that is standard and meets their needs. If we are hoping to add new programs or change something from past practices, the teams will create items on the survey to address the proposed changes. If we are unsure, we should contact a district-level person, or a master colleague for suggestions.

Survival Tips

♦ *Create a setting that promotes the importance of a schoolwide plan for improvement.* If we want to create the feeling that we are going to improve student and teacher performance, then provide an atmosphere that demonstrates the importance of collaborating on a new and better school plan.

♦ *Don't rush the process.* As stated earlier, it takes a full year to complete the process of developing a schoolwide plan when everyone becomes involved in the initial stages.

♦ *Recognize that we work with two plans at a time.* When school begins we already put in place a plan to chart the course for the current year. The improvement plan described in this book becomes the guidelines for the upcoming year.

Summary

Solutions to problems should remain fluid because of the variables that occur throughout the year "The practice of reviewing data, making midcourse corrections, and focusing decision making on the greatest points of leverage—is superior to 'neat' leadership in which planning, processes, and procedures take precedence over achievement…. The keys are monitoring, evaluation, values, beliefs, and implementation" (Reeves, 2006, p. xi).

How does a purposeful principal make sure that the faculty will live by the statements they made in a school plan? The elusive buy-in we need requires serious dedication on our part.

- We continuously remind faculty, students, and parents how everyone demonstrates their commitment to the school plan.
- Faculty members hear consistently from the administrative group and problem-solving team members, how much everyone values the work of each contributing faculty and parent member.

In summary, the amount of time we spend identifying schoolwide goals with the entire faculty depends on the level; elementary, middle, or high school; the size of the faculty; the complexity of the problems. For purposes of the schoolwide faculty meeting only the most relevant information that affects all teachers requires presentation at this time.

It is all about us as school leaders. Our total commitment, passion, and belief in the mission, vision, values, and goals become evident in our interaction with all the groups that support us. They support us because we support them. School leaders emerge during times like this. We will continuously connect with the faculty problem-solving team as well as the additional school leaders we identified. They help spread the word about where the school is going and why.

As the school leader we analyze the behavior of each of the stakeholders as they participate in the activity. We will find the leaders. Where is everyone else? Questions arise in our quest to find out. Is someone acting detached from the process? Why? Who is very involved and appears interested in participating? Who did not show up for the process in spite of our request? Why? Who are the cheerleaders for the vision? Who are the naysayers? Who really "gets it?" Information provided by observing how faculty members participate in the process will help us and our administrative team craft conferences when teachers discuss their individual goals.

The importance of a plan can not be undervalued. A plan is no more than a written document with meaningless words unless the purpose of the plan becomes the focus and not just the document for document's sake. Plans are messy.

As school teams become committed to the mission, vision, values, and goals, then different approaches emerge. Problem-solving ideas develop from any position: teacher; student; administrative team; faculty problem-solving team; committee members; department or grade-level chairs; office staff; and custodians.

Making Connections

An earlier example of schoolwide goals required that teachers make moral decisions. Even though not everyone understood how they would "teach reading" they agreed as a school it was important. They would become part of learning new ideas.

As school leaders we recognize the ethical obligations we have to improve student scores. We have the moral and ethical responsibility to the faculty to approach a new instructional process slowly and methodically, with a carefully developed plan.

Application

♦ Discuss the moral issues that could emerge from the need for the faculty to agree on a schoolwide plan.

♦ What ethical decisions occur when the district mandates an instructional requirement and the teachers, as a whole, do not think it makes sense?

♦ When decisions occur where the school leader must make a decision between what is either morally or ethically the "right thing to do," which value wins?

♦ Discuss examples of moral and ethical dilemmas that would affect an entire school and their plans for improvement.

♦ In what situations would we make decisions that affected the entire school that was neither moral nor ethical?

"For a school to be more than a loose confederation of independent learning environments, all stakeholders must be clear on the beliefs that give collective and concrete purpose to their individual efforts."

—Zmuda, Kuklis, and Kline (2004, p. 40).

5

Purposeful Individual Goal Setting: Finding the Needs

Individual goals require purposeful identification and motivation to ensure that each faculty member clearly identifies steps in an individualized process to accomplish them. When, as the school leader, we provide each faculty member with the foundational skills, opportunity for reflection, and a clearly identified support system, individual goals become a powerful commitment for improved performance. This requires a system that organizes teacher needs, determines who will support those needs, and provides necessary resources.

The faculty of the new millennium identifies and recognizes the mission, vision, values, and goals through the lenses of moral and ethical leadership. The knowledge base from which to draw their own conclusions on ways to improve their own and student learning goes to a much deeper level.

It requires patience, time, and a clearly identified process so that each faculty member understands the expectations and purpose of their plans. It requires a process that accommodates the needs of individual teachers to create a scaffolding approach for successful achievement.

The example used in this chapter explains a way to get everyone started on the individual goal-setting process at the same time. It begins when faculty members commit to the goal or goals they identified in the first part of their individual plan. Information gathered during this time provides a process to plan staff development (chapter 6). The final part of the plan is written at the first staff development session.

Teachers began creating individual goals years ago. What is different, and how can we, as school leaders, provide the incentive for the stakeholders to understand the value of their personal commitment to the organization and to improve student and teacher performance? Staff members need both short-term and long-term goals. Most of all, a specific plan for continuous review and reflection emphasizes the value we place on the process.

"Back in the day" when curriculum, instruction, and assessment were based on single textbooks, driven by intermittent exams on the content, goals became something the district required. Eventually, the process, in many schools, deteriorated to a "just do it" process.

Unfortunately, it is still not uncommon in schools for teachers to write a plan and put it aside until the principal asks for it at the end of the year. Perhaps a conscientious administrator held a midyear conference, and the principal signed off on the plan and placed it in a file, never to be seen again. Additional members of the staff such as the visual and performing arts, physical education, media specialists, and others who did not have core content subjects to teach were often exempt from writing goals, or the goals lacked substance. Why such a lax attitude about such an important process? Many school leaders tell us that it takes too much time. Time they don't have to give.

When this happens, the importance of committing to specific areas of individual improvement becomes undervalued and deteriorates to another annoying piece of paperwork to complete. The school leader, the administrative support group, and the faculty problem-solving team become the first line of reinforcement to ensure each faculty members feels valued for their important role in accomplishing their goal.

When Do I Begin?

As soon as the entire faculty agrees on the mission and purpose, vision, values, and schoolwide goals, the next steps in the process occur. We may choose to complete the process from chapters 4 through 6 in a one-half day session prior to the opening of school. We may decide to use three or four one-hour sessions during the first month of school. The examples below assume three different meetings.

Note: If we select to complete the process in one half-day session, then we would eliminate some of the recommended steps. For example, we would not have time to compile the moral, ethical, and values beliefs as well as the mission/purpose and vision statements. The charts would remain visible and compiling of the information would occur at a later time.

What Should I Do and How Should I Do It?

The Administrative Team

Preliminary Steps: Review the Schoolwide Goals Setting Process

Step 1: After the schoolwide faculty meeting, we meet with the administrative support team to review the conclusions reached by the faculty. The administrative groups and faculty problem-solving team retrieve the charts from the table groups and consolidate the statements.

We assign editors to write statements that reflect the mission and purpose, vision, values, and schoolwide goals. This provides the faculty with the substance to build their individual goals.

Step 2: The administrative team creates a system to identify the areas in which teachers need support; from whom will they receive that support and to what degree? What questions need answering before we plan staff development described in chapter 6?

- Does the schoolwide goal affect every member of the staff? If so, then a large staff development plan is needed.

- Does the schoolwide goal affect each faculty member or small group in different ways? If small groups have similar needs, then staff development becomes individualized.

- Before teachers begin planning their goals, how much money can we commit for staff development?

- How much money is available for staff development; particularly for hiring substitutes to give teachers time to plan?

- What can we provide in the form of staff development options? If we place any limitations on the available resources, we need to let the faculty know right up front.

The administrative group identifies ways to coordinate the needs of the teachers, and the support requested, compared to the available money. As school leader we want a direct connection between the needs of individuals and increased improvement in adult and student learning (Guskey, 1999).

The teams create a workable survey. The following hypothetical discussion may serve as examples for a starting point and explain the thinking that could occur among the team members (administrative support team or faculty problem-solving team).

- ♦ At the schoolwide faculty meeting, when the faculty heard about our absentee numbers, they listed this as an important goal; reduce the number of absences. This does not affect every teacher. This will become a goal for only some teachers.
  - A discussion should occur concerning the specific teachers who experience high absentee rates and identify the underlying causes before implementing specific suggestions on ways to assist.
  - This requires specific direction to those teachers involved concerning an identified target when writing his or her goal.
- ♦ A schoolwide goal based on lack of identified progress in reading: reading across the curriculum. This affects every teacher; but in different ways. What can we provide in the way of services, staff support, and time that would help a teacher with reading in his or her subject area?
- ♦ A schoolwide goal: teachers will teach students to solve problems and make decisions through critical, creative, and conceptual thinking.
- ♦ Is this a new concept for all teachers? If so, then a schoolwide plan for staff development requires an expert to provide the background for all teachers. Writing individual goals to learn a new concept requires a teacher to think about what they know, what they need to know, how they intend to learn, and how they will know if they learned it.
  - Is there an in-school expert?
  - Is there a credible expert at the district level that could provide the needed background?
  - If no one in the school district is available, is there enough money to bring in an outside consultant?
  - Is there another school with which we could share expenses?

The point of the above examples relates to a clear understanding of the key stakeholder's needs and the realistic approaches that could provide faculty members with support. We must only provide options that are possible and practical. This may require limiting the number or complexity of the goal based on realistic targets that would ensure success on the part of each faculty member.

As the principal we will determine available finances before we let teachers assume that, once they identify their need, it becomes a done deal. For example, unless our resources provide enough money to send teachers to conferences, do not offer that as an option. A teacher, who believes the best way to improve his or her teaching means attending the reading conference in Hawaii, should recognize the budget limitations for conference attendance. During this part of the questionnaire, a set of options provides teachers with the support available that become doable according to the financial availability. We may decide to provide a list of the options up front.

The complexity of the goal and the skill level of the teacher will determine if we recommend limiting the number of goals any individual teacher will attempt to accomplish.

Preliminary Goal Setting

The Invitation

During our staff meeting on (date) we will continue the process of examining our plan to help with school improvement. We will identify the schoolwide goal or goals we selected and decide the type of staff development support we need.

As a school we identified the following goal or goals needed for improved student performance:

_____

(List them)

Once again, our administrative support group and the problem-solving team facilitate small groups. We organize table groups according to possible areas of common interest: new teachers, veteran teachers, teams, or groups.

Teachers receive the entire document that they created and the team synthesized. Each faculty member will receive the following statements created in charts, posters, or some visual (to place in each room and remain visible to everyone).

The focus	School specific graphics/text
◆ Purpose and mission	graphics/ text here
◆ Ethical and moral beliefs	graphics/text here
◆ Vision	graphics/text here

- Values   graphics/text here
- Schoolwide goal   graphics/text here

As school leader we could say: "During this session we will identify the schoolwide goal or goals as our area of concentration. Then, we will brainstorm with the table facilitator the support we need to ensure our success. In that way, we can organize into small groups and identify common areas of support for staff development. It is not expected that we complete the dates, activities, or assessment plans at this time. All of the details for individual plans will occur during the first staff development session."

The facilitator provides suggestions and serves as a support for the teacher when determining workable and achievable goals. The facilitator also serves as a "voice of reason" in case teachers see no point in writing goals with purpose and a commitment to the schoolwide plan. This also prevents teachers from going off in a totally different direction from the initial intent of the schoolwide plan. (Save this opportunity for the master teachers described in chapter 6.)

If this goal-setting process is new to the teachers, the facilitator could brainstorm ideas in case they need suggestions concerning writing goals and understanding the opportunities for support. The members of the problem-solving team would facilitate discussions as faculty members examine options for individual goal concentration.

An example of a discussion could include:

The art teacher states:

- I want to understand ways to incorporate reading strategies into everyday practice in the teaching of art (Schoolwide goal: Reading across the curriculum.)

The music and math teacher want a common goal:

- We want to work together and create vocabulary words, develop strategies of instruction, and help students understand the critical connection between the language of music and mathematics. (Schoolwide goal: Reading across the curriculum.)

The social studies team of five wants to work together on the same goal:

- Our team wants to learn more effective strategies for teaching students how to solve problems and make decisions and ask higher-order questions within the content of our textbook. (Schoolwide goal: provide students with opportunities to solve problems through creative, critical, and conceptual thinking.)

The following example provides suggestions for the table group leader in order to assist members of the faculty. (See Figure 5.1 on page 96 for a blank teacher survey.)

Mission:

Vision: *Provide the agreed-on statements*

Values: *from the schoolwide planning meeting.*

Schoolwide goals:
- improve attendance (affects only some of the faculty)
- provide reading across the curriculum (affects all)
- provide students with opportunities to solve problems through creative, critical, and conceptual thinking (affects all)

Teacher Name _____ Grade level or department _____

Which goal or goals will you incorporate into your individual plan?

Examples:

Goal 1. I will provide students with opportunities to solve problems through creative, critical, and conceptual thinking.

Why did you select this particular goal? (What did the data show?)

Goal 1. My students did not do as well on the standardized test as I thought they should. I believe it is because I don't provide them enough opportunities for higher-order thinking. So they don't think beyond the facts.

How will you accomplish your goal?

Goal 1. I need training on higher-order questioning.
          I need to learn about teaching conceptually.
          I will develop methods of presenting students with problems to solve or decisions to make using higher-order, critical, and conceptual thinking.

Figure 5.1.
Preliminary Staff Survey–Identification of Desired Goals

The following survey will identify those school-wide goals that you identified during the faculty meeting on __(date)__ that will help you hone your craft of teaching while assisting students in learning at higher levels.

Once you complete your goals we will gather the information and begin determining appropriate staff development options. As you consider your goal or goals, determine the best support we can provide you.

Applying your goals to the school's mission/purpose and values will provide a seamless flow through to your individual goals.

A member of the faculty problem-solving team will assist you if you have questions concerning the expectations. Your goal statements will be handed to the team member before you leave today. In this way, we can begin establishing our support to you.

Mission: Statements are taken from the schoolwide faculty meeting

Vision:

Values:

Schoolwide goals:

Teacher Name _____ Grade level or department _____

Explain each goal, that you determined will support the statements above. (If you are a first or second year teachers, or a teacher new to our school, limit yourself to one goal.) Veteran teachers may want more than one goal.

For each goal complete the following information:

Why did you select this particular goal? (What did the data show?)

In order to support you in your goal, what do you need in the form of resources?

What are your preliminary plans for assessing your student's progress as you develop your goal?

In order to support you with your goal, what do you need in the form of resources?

Goal 1.

_____ I need a coach who can come into my room and see how I can improve.

_____ I need to go into other teacher's classrooms and watch them use higher-order questioning techniques.

_____ I need to read more; work with other teachers and talk about how to ask the right questions to the right students?

_____ I need complete training by an expert. I have no idea what I am supposed to do because the concept is completely new to me.

_____ I would like to have a day with my team to determine the best approaches I can use to meet my goal.

_____ Any other options the school could actually provide.

Goals are not completed at this time, only the commitment to implement one or more of them with the identified support needed. Only when the surveys are analyzed will the administrative team know the staff development needed. Then, the individual plans become completed during the first staff development meeting.

When the facilitator determines that each member of the table group completes the survey, the administrative team collects the preliminary goals. When all goals are completed at the same time, the administrative group begins consolidating the information.

Gathering, Compiling, and Drawing Initial Conclusions From the Survey

Collecting a survey, signing it, and assuming the faculty members will improve their teaching practices and at the same time improve student learning wastes everyone's time. Purposeful goals require careful assessment of each teacher's skill level, attitude, experience, and commitment to personal and student learning gains. Planning for meaningful staff development (chapter 6) requires examination of each of these components.

Determine potential groupings of teachers who identify similar goals and the support needed. For example: We find that more than one teacher would like to participate in the same activity. Several want to learn about reading across the curriculum; teams want to work together to learn how to teach at a conceptual level. A large group wants to investigate questioning. Groups form through analyzing needs in a variety of ways.

With the administrative team, identify the competence level of each teacher. It will make a difference on the type of staff development provided. Although several teachers want to learn ways to instruct using higher-order questioning, do all members of the group have the same knowledge base or content background?

One Size Does Not Fit All

As leader, we will identify other groups unique to our particular school. The following examples provide ideas:

- Novice: New teachers; zero to three years experience
- Apprentice: four to five years experience
- Master teachers: Those who meet the criteria described later in this chapter
- Special needs teachers: Those who function at a novice level but have more experience. They probably operate with a previous special improvement plan and require specific attention.

Novice Teachers and Individual Plans

Teachers with one to three years experience still struggle. They function best when they identify a goal that provides small incremental steps, where success becomes easily recognized. They will participate with their team if we provide planning days for them. During that time they learn by listening and asking questions as the discussion evolves.

A novice needs continuous support and attention from a capable colleague. However, the concentration still occurs with one area, in baby steps, toward feeling successful.

For example, assume the novice does not understand how to teach reading in the content areas. Focus on one content area such as social studies. Introduce one strategy at a time for the novice to listen, observe, try in the classroom, and reflect with the coach; assist them in understanding how the integration of reading skills and concepts crosses the curriculum.

Novice teachers also focus on assessing the strategy used. Frequently, new teachers try something out; pray it worked, push ahead without mastering one strategy at a time or assessing to validate progress. This emphasis becomes the coach's responsibility to identify strategies for quick and accurate assessment concerning student progress so the teacher receives immediate feedback. Slow and steady, with realistic expectations concerning progress, create an atmosphere for success.

The facilitator will recognize the novice and guide him or her toward writing very concrete goals with detailed timelines to accomplish one goal. Less is more with the novice.

The Apprentice

Teachers with four years experience or more begin demonstrating their levels of competence. (Some shining stars demonstrate the competencies as an apprentice by their third year.) What are the characteristics of an apprentice level teacher?

♦ Diversity of skills and knowledge exists among these teachers.

♦ This group becomes clearer about what they want and need to learn.

♦ They often recognize colleagues with similar interests. They will likely identify goals within their groups. They are familiar with the school culture.

♦ They exhibit metacognitive skills; they know what they don't know and they know how to find ways to improve.

♦ This group requires recognition. This is the time, according to research, when most teachers leave the profession. They require particular support as they work to achieve the identified goals.

The downside of apprentice teachers: they often become fragmented as their interests become diversified. The good news: typically these teachers think of a variety of ways to accomplish the goals. The assessment piece often provides the most conversation and ideas. The facilitator knows the more experienced teachers at their table group and keeps them focused on the schoolwide goals.

The apprentice could identify more than one goal; they may want to coach each other. They need to carefully and methodically develop a substantive plan, complete with accountability throughout the year. Since this is typically the largest group, consistent checking to see how the goal is progressing becomes a key element among the members of the administrative support team.

This group will divide into several teams depending on the specific strategies needed to accomplish their goals. The majority of teachers on a typical team fall into the apprentice range. Of course, it depends on the school.

The Master Teacher

Master teachers provide the backbone of the school. The administrative team observes the master teacher demonstrating a level of competence both in and out of the classroom. What are their characteristics?

- They know and understand the mission and purpose, vision, and values of the school. They create and utilize curriculum, instruction, and assessment based on those beliefs.
- They willingly help the school leader. They serve a valuable function on the faculty problem-solving team.
- They "know their stuff." We watch them work their magic and hear it in the responses by students when in their classrooms.
- They are experienced with five or more years in the classroom.
- When analyzing individual testing data, these teachers demonstrate impressive gains for their students. If every student does not meet the teacher's expectations, they give a logical explanation.
- Formal and authentic assessment drives their instruction.
- They think deeply about what they do, analyzing continuously.
- They contribute effectively when solving problems.
- School leaders and colleagues respect and value their opinions.
- They objectively look at the big picture.
- They read professional literature to find better ways to do their job.
- They get along with others; they lead gently.
- Their standardized test scores continue to improve at impressive rates.

The master teacher understands how to reach the identified school goals. In many cases they figured out the issues long before the formal data emerged. Most of the time they have "been there, done that." They continually improve their craft without establishing a formal goal. They find the more complex schoolwide options and increase their competence. This is the teacher who will determine better questioning strategies and learn more effective ways to develop and present critical, creative, and conceptual thinking. In this way they are minimally challenged. Chapter six describes optional plans for the master teacher, beyond an already-mastered schoolwide goal.

Special Needs Teachers

Previous assessments, observations, and lack of student progress identify special needs teachers. They exhibit similar characteristics:

♦ They see no reason to improve their instructional practices; they see themselves as doing just fine.

♦ They often want to be left alone; interaction with others more competent just frustrates them.

♦ They agree, go through the required motions to develop goals, then close their classroom doors and go about doing what they have always done, getting the same results.

♦ They exhibit passive aggressive behaviors; often griping and whining to others without addressing the "real problem."

♦ They are often high maintenance, taking enormous amounts of time with colleagues and administrators, with few positive outcomes.

♦ They choose not to handle change of any kind.

♦ They resent writing goals; they feel they are a waste of time since they already know what they are doing.

The special needs teacher requires concentrated effort when participating in goal-writing sessions. As the leader we pay particular attention to their involvement in the process. Once the survey of goals and needs is completed and handed in to the administrative support team we read them carefully. Are the goals focused on specific areas to improve based on the schoolwide decisions? Does the survey indicate a token attempt at doing what they "have to do"?

The challenge for the school leader: how much time and effort should we expect to devote to a teacher who refuses to work with us in any substantive way? This is an issue to discuss early with our administrative team. The special needs teacher usually exhibits commitment, or lack thereof, to the improvement process during schoolwide and goal-setting meetings.

Ancillary Staff

Although we may not require custodians, food service staff, and the office personnel to write down academic goals, they should become part of the schoolwide effort to improve student learning. Create an opportunity for them to feel part of the whole process. Ancillary staff should be provided the opportunity to contribute to schoolwide goals whenever possible. A facilitator would assist them during the planning meeting.

- ◆ How could they assist with reading across the curriculum?
  - These groups interact with students consistently. Discuss the schoolwide goal of reading across the curriculum and ask for ideas they may generate concerning ways they could reinforce reading.

    The food service staff may identify several ways to support the application of reading. Menus are posted for students to read. Lunchroom rules are generally posted in most schools; students read those.

- ◆ What ideas could emerge when discussing students who arrive at school late?
  - The custodian may volunteer to mentor one of more chronically late students. He or she makes an agreement to greet the student every morning.
  - A food service person agrees to pay special attention to another consistently tardy student.

- ◆ The office staff often volunteers to listen to students at the elementary level, read to them as a reward from the teacher.
  - In middle and high school, the office staff often asks students to read documents and forms, interpreting for non-English speaking parents and students.

Questions and Answers

Q: Why expect all faculty members to come together one more time. Why not just hand them a form, expect them to complete it, and hand it in?

A1: If we ask the teachers to complete a simple form at a staff meeting, we will get one back from everyone. The facilitator reviews the goals at that time. They hand us their goal and the resources the teacher requests before they leave the meeting. In this way the administrative team can look it over and determine the quality of his/her goal and if it meets our expectations. In addition, we will determine if their need for support is something meaningful and doable. This process ensures that each faculty member recognizes the importance of his/her personal role and our commitment to provide support.

With the information provided, we can effectively plan staff development.

A2: If we expect teachers to hand back forms in a timely manner, good luck. In this way, everyone begins the process. Once we get everyone started, then the completion for the rest of the plan occurs during the first staff development meeting.

Q: How long does the process take from the point when we discuss moral and ethical beliefs to this time when teachers begin identifying their schoolwide goals?

A1: A well-organized administrative and problem-solving team, who completed the rehearsal, can complete the entire process in about four hours.

A2: We want to begin staff development as soon as possible in the year, so we must start early. The most efficient method occurs if we provide planning time before the school year begins, such as one-half day during preplanning (see Survival Tips).

Q: As principal or assistant principal, do I need to participate through the whole session? I am so busy.

A: Yes. We set the tone. If we are not present, the staff will be present in body only. Our enthusiasm and personal interest in the faculty's involvement will determine the overall success of goal setting.

Q: Why involve everyone in the plan? Why not just get the problem-solving team or some other group together and write it? The rest of the staff wouldn't care.

A: This is a common way to develop a plan. One group understands the mission of the school and everyone else complains because they don't. As stated earlier, everyone needs to own the plan. Therefore, everyone needs to create it, together.

Survival Tips

♦ *Create a list of any limitations that exist when the faculty begins thinking of staff development options.* Generally, this is money related. No, there is no money for conferences. We only have money to buy time. How much time? Let them know. If one teacher receives two days for planning and another one only gets one, we know what that means. If we have money for every teacher to receive two days of planning, then reveal any criteria attached. There is enough money for every teacher to receive a substitute in the classroom for two days. This is available only to those teachers who are part of a group of four or more who have a common staff development need.

Whatever the criteria, whatever the limitations the decision rests with the school leader. What is the moral and ethical thing to do? Let everyone know the rules.

♦ *Why should we try to complete the entire process of developing a school plan in a half day session before school starts* (assuming the district allows that option)? The good news: this is a very efficient way to get everyone together without separating out the process over three or four different meetings. The bad news: If we did not inform the faculty well in advance of the plan, we could be in a lot of trouble. The good news: If in the welcoming back letter, sent at least one month before the start of school, we provide an agenda of the activities prior to school opening, at least we prepared them.

♦ *Create a system to identify information we need to determine staff development options.* An example:

Teacher Name	Proficiency Level	Topic of Their Goal	Number of Hours/Days Needed	Cost	Support Person(s)
Perez, M.	Novice	Reading in social studies	40 Hours/ 6 months	0	Peer Coach
			Team Planning 2 days	formula	1 day district-level social studies teacher

Summary

The value of teachers committing to individual goals rests in the ability to keep the school focused. Individual goals connect directly to schoolwide goals. Granted, there are many things to do and many issues to solve, but schools are too complex an organization to rush the process.

Staff development (chapter 6) occurs from the needs of the teacher. Every teacher does not create an individualized plan. From the administrative perspective, that becomes unmanageable. Rather, small groups form when collective interests emerge from discussing and identifying their individual needs. Through the conversations with others, teachers find shared areas of interest to explore. This is the basis for collaboration; not forced on the faculty, but discovered through common goals.

Short-term goals provide immediate response to the teacher to see if the strategy works, allowing quick midcourse corrections when needed. Long-term goals provide a way to look at the anticipated final outcome and work backward. Both types are necessary. Intermediate steps require collaboration with others for additional suggestions and ideas. Those involved in supporting others need a plan, identified dates for discussion, and time provided to assist in making the approach better.

It is up to us and all other members of the faculty, students, and parents, to support the uninterested, nurture the reluctant ones, and celebrate those who "carry the torch" on behalf of the school's mission, vision, values, and goals.

The importance of a plan can not be undervalued. A plan is no more than a written document with meaningless words unless the purpose of the plan becomes the focus and not just the document for document's sake. Plans are messy. They change continuously as additional variables infiltrate a school.

Making Connections

As school leader, we have both a moral and ethical obligation to support teachers in achieving their goals; otherwise, why put everyone through the time consuming task? The purpose of helping teachers improve their craft becomes fundamental to overall student achievement (chapter 6).

When teachers make decisions on how to improve, they too make decisions based on their morals, ethics, and values. We express enthusiasm and support for each of the teachers based on the individual or small group needs, the message is clear. Together, we make the mission, vision, and values of the school work.

Faculty members who feel supported work harder. The individual attention paid to establishing goals and celebrating accomplishments establishes a pattern. The administrative group values the effort staff members put into improving their instruction.

Application

♦   Identify a system to ensure continuous reflection and monitoring of teacher goals. Why is it important?

- What moral and ethical issues did teachers and the administrators experience in this chapter?

- How would we evaluate the process described in this chapter if a school becomes one that focuses on its mission, vision, values, and goals?

- Discuss the advantages and disadvantages of the process in this chapter. What would we do to accomplish the same objective so that everyone will own the plan?

Effective decision making when moral and ethical considerations exist are best described by Robert Greenleaf (1977). He describes an effective leader as one who can say, "we know where we are, where we have been, and where we are going—all in the context as large and complete as we can construct and understand" (p. 148).

"The great danger for most of us is not that our aim is too high and we miss it, but that it is too low and we reach it."

—Michelangelo

6

Differentiated Staff Development

Traditional staff development, a one-size-fits-all approach, does not meet the individual needs of teachers. Rather than assume that staff development will improve the skills and strategies for all teachers the same way, evaluation of the most effective plan is based on individual or small group needs.

Create staff development experiences that acknowledge and accommodate the different needs of teachers much the same way as teachers develop strategies to differentiate classroom instruction. In addition, faculty members relate staff development to the individual commitment to the mission, purpose, vision, and values through the lenses of moral and ethical leadership.

Faculty members identified common areas of interest in chapter 5. The focus rests on improving individual performance for themselves and their students. From this discussion, differentiated staff development emerges.

This chapter provides suggestions for appropriate and meaningful training for individuals and small groups to accomplish their identified goals. In addition, discussion and suggestions occur concerning the master teacher. Master teachers deserve special consideration to help each of them grow professionally. Staff development for that group of teachers requires a separate discussion in this chapter.

To focus the discussion on differentiated staff development, the school goals cited in earlier chapters will continue as examples. Each of the ideas suggested becomes a way to target individual staff development plans. Creating a staff development plan begins with the individual teacher's need, defines how to improve his/her performance in a way that directly impacts student learning, and reinforces the school goals. Each plan is written according to district guidelines. Individuals determine their own staff development options.

As suggestions for differentiated staff development follow, the continuous thread toward faculty and staff improvement remains focused on critical questions. As school leader we answer:

♦ How will we provide time and support for teachers?

♦ Are dates identified on the school calendar that describe when the faculty meets in small groups to ensure that continues discussion occurs throughout the year?

♦ What is the individual's plan to increase personal and student performance based on the school goal or goals?

♦ How will each faculty member and administrator contribute to his/ her own and other's understanding of strategies to progress effectively on a continuum of learning?

♦ Finally, what proof determines realization of the goal?

Schoolwide Staff Development

Schoolwide staff development occurs under limited circumstances. When an entire staff receives a presentation affecting every member of the faculty, this must mean a change in existing practices. Preliminary discussions with our administrative group, the faculty problem-solving team, and small group discussions precede this event.

If our public relations groups (those who understand the mission, vision, values, and purpose) within the school "infected" their colleagues with the importance and potential benefits of learning how to do something in a better way, staff development proceeds effectively. The staff development must accomplish three things: (1) It is practical for everyone; (2) there is perceived value for the teacher's time; and (3) it supports a schoolwide goal.

This approach makes sense when a new idea or method is introduced. For example, the schoolwide goal stated that students will learn to solve problems through creative, critical, and conceptual thinking. Although teachers agreed that students need to make critical connections across the content areas and think at higher levels, all faculty members lack consistent background information.

Faculty members need to make their own connections between what they know, their current practices, and how to implement the new goal. They need to understand the common language for higher-order conceptual thinking.

Who presents the new concept? For example, if concept-based integrated units of instruction are generated at the district level as Erickson (2006) recommends, then someone from the staff likely served on the districtwide writing team. That representative, and ideally, someone from the district writing team, best describe the background, process, and intended outcomes. When two people present the same information with the entire administrative team present, faculty members take it seriously. Following the presentation, each faculty member receives a summary of the key points.

Progressive school districts provide enough money for principals to generate time to train teachers who serve as "on-site experts." In this way, a common vocabulary becomes reinforced as discussions occur across grade levels. Teachers use similar terms to describe their instructional strategies. The school "expert," the administrative support group, and the faculty problem-solving team help each person understand ways to reach the new school goal.

Identifying each teacher's needs and current proficiency level provides us with planning individual and small group options. Differentiated staff development becomes the most viable possibility in order to create successful implementation of school goals.

Questions to answer:

- What developmental level exists for each teacher? As a school leader, how is that level determined? How will the staff development accommodate the different levels of understanding?
- What resources are available?
- Who will coach and assess the progress of each group?

Developmental Levels of the Faculty Revisited

For purposes of explanation and clarity, the developmental levels of teachers are revisited again from chapter 5, from the perspective of identifying staff development options. This recognizes that identifying single categories of teachers remains in flux just as groupings of students change continuously. There occurs a wide range of abilities within each grouping. Overlapping of competence and crossover of categories occurs naturally, just as it occurs in classrooms.

Developmental levels of staff occur on a continuum of understanding when implementing the agreed-on goals. The examples assume the faculty members demonstrate the desire to improve. How many years of successful experience did the teacher exhibit? Underachieving teachers occur in the category of special needs teachers.

Supporting the Novice: 0-3 Years Experience

Beginning teachers barely keep their heads above water, let alone embark on complex tasks of learning something for which they have no prior experiences or knowledge. As much as we may want a brand new teacher to hit the ground running, understand the culture, and teach using creative innovative ideas, it rarely happens.

Compounding the issue, more and more teachers (particularly in ever-expanding districts) enter teaching without a formal teaching background. This group requires extensive support.

School leaders understand that the inexperienced teacher needs direct instruction, just as the student who begins learning a new concept. The support requires specific, uncomplicated strategies and guidelines. The new teacher requires the same scaffolding techniques of any learner, with the guidance of a master.

Staff development requires one-on-one support to learn the culture of the school from a mentor. A coach provides small incremental steps toward learning one school goal at a time. Together with the coach and administrators, we reach common agreement on what that one piece looks like; this becomes their staff development. Spare them the frustration of attending staff development sessions that put them way over their heads. Without the critical connections between what they know and what we expect them to apply in their instruction, we waste their precious time.

Second year teachers are still learning the culture although they acquired a beginning background from which to develop. This novice is not as dependent on the mentor, but still needs assistance. The mentor reduces their number of responsibilities (assuming the teacher still teaches the same grade level and demonstrates personal improvement and motivation to learn) as the novice becomes more comfortable with the management pieces of the job.

The coach takes on a role to help move the teacher toward improving his or her craft. Selecting one schoolwide goal, with an in-depth, albeit still baby-step plan to improve, provides a greater opportunity for successful implementation. This is the beginning of the end of some teacher's careers in education. They need mentoring, coaching, small incremental steps toward improving, and feelings of continuous success.

Third year teachers, much like the master teachers, often are the neglected ones. After all, it seems as if they should have it all figured out by now. Unfortunately, many third year teachers think they have it all figured out as well. Traditionally, attention to mentoring and coaching third year teachers is eliminated. Why?

Most evaluations that determine tenured status occur at the end of the third year. Teachers feel that pressure. This is the time when, according to the literature, teachers leave the profession. The reason cited: not enough support. Assume that it isn't the lack of support, but rather the lack of continuous support through the first three years. Much like we move students too quickly through the curriculum, going a mile wide and an inch deep. Do we move teachers too quickly; expecting too much too soon?

The third year teacher knows the questions to ask that brings greater clarity to his/her instructional strategies. Staff development for the third year teacher becomes more sophisticated. We provide them with experiences among apprentice and master teachers based on their desire to improve in identified areas that support the school goals.

Staff Development Options

Staff development is focused first on those who need foundational skills. The beginning teacher needs support from two different sources; a mentor and a coach. Some apprentice-level teachers, interested in helping, provide assistance to the school leader in fulfilling the role of mentor.

Creating a staff development plan requires collaboration among both support members and the novice teacher. The mentor and coach collaborate and find common meeting times. Together, they all determine how best to provide for the needs of the new teacher. The differing roles will be discussed in detail later in this chapter.

True Story

I watched in horror as a newly hired teacher returned to her classroom from a team meeting loaded to her chin with cross-stacked piles of worksheets. When I asked where the worksheets came from she answered, "The team thought I should have work for the students who either finished their work early, or who needed extra practice." To which I replied, "Do we know what you will do with all that paper?" "No, they were trying to help me out, but I am so confused about what to do with it all." I took the papers from her. "I will send your mentor and coach to help you."

—Elementary principal

The Leader's Role

Find the best possible matches for the novice teacher for two areas of support: one to mentor and one to coach. The rationale for two support people comes from the need to value the time mentors and coaches need for their own professional development.

Meet with the novice group and their coaches to help guide the beginning teacher in developing realistic goals. They need to hear from us as leaders, concerning our expectations and based on the logical expectation for their success along a continuum of skill development.

Ask about the agreed-on times that they will meet.

Supporting the Apprentice: 4-5 Years Experience

By the time a faculty member reaches this level of experience, the teacher should demonstrate a fairly high level of competence. Staff development for this group becomes very substantive. Targets for school improvement become well defined. Apprentice individuals and groups understand the basic curriculum, instruction, and assessment components. They know the culture of the school.

They now expand on what they know and develop critical, creative, and conceptual thinking about how to advance their own understanding; moving themselves "beyond the facts" (Erickson, 2006). Not until faculty members experience higher-order thinking on a personal level, through up-leveling individual staff development, will they develop the foundational skills to provide students the same opportunity.

Individual metacognitive ability becomes more acute. Apprentice teachers understand the areas on which they need to concentrate in order to improve their instruction and assessments. They are ready to expand their knowledge base with greater conceptual understanding and creativity. They now know what they don't know, and they know who to ask for help in "fixing it."

Although teachers in all three experience groups require differentiation due to their ability, motivation, and instincts, some small group staff development can occur. As Tomlinson and McTighe (2006) point out in their insights concerning differentiated instruction; it isn't practical or possible to individualize every student's learning every step of the way.

Natural leaders emerge from this group. They cluster more easily due to their similar learning curves and background of experiences. In a collaborative setting, faculty members meet to identify the best strategies for implementing the goals with clearly defined steps on reaching them.

Keeping apprentice-level teachers focused requires guidance from us as leaders. This group needs encouragement to perfect their instructional skills, grasp the concepts that raise their level of sophistication in accomplishing their goals. This group could become our next level of master teachers.

Staff Development Options

Coach

- This assumes there is truth to the adage, "When we teach we learn twice." If that is the case, then training an apprentice to assume mentoring and coaching rolls becomes a way to scaffold the coach's own learning. Skills to accomplish a coaching role require specific training with a clear set of expectations and support for everyone involved.

- They support the novice with instructional strategies (from the agreed-on goals).

- They learn to scaffold the novice teacher's learning experiences.

- If an apprentice demonstrates the ability to support others, as school leader, provide staff development time to "learn to coach." The subset then becomes: learning to coach a novice toward reaching the school goal. The coach and assigned novice identify a specific strategy to implement with focused, single activities to ensure success for themselves and their students.

- A coach begins by helping the novice apply organizational management from the mentor's suggestions to the application part of classroom management (the most difficult piece for the first year teacher). Without structure for the students, nothing else happens.

- Meeting the schoolwide goal occurs in much smaller steps than with the apprentice and master teachers. The coach will break down the skills needed for the teacher to implement one strategy at a time. The novice will continue to work improving his or her own learning, while increasing student understanding of the identified concepts.

- The coach applauds small successes while providing year-long assistance.

- Skilled coaches understand the importance of scaffolding a beginning teacher's experiences in curriculum, instruction, and assessment.

- Protect the novice from well-meaning colleagues who assume that their treasured black-line master copies of worksheets that probably predate the Revolutionary War provide the important instructional supplemental work "at least to keep the kids under control."

- The staff development plan for the novice should remain fluid. Rather than determine all possibilities for attaining improvement, start with one step. When that is accomplished, the coach will help the novice develop the next step and so on. Document one step at a time, one success at a time.

♦ Textbooks written in the last three years contain enough information on what to do and how to do it, that the coach can provide reassurance that by following "the book" there is little room for error. Textbooks provide more information than a teacher needs. The problem for the novice teacher comes in not knowing what not to worry about.

♦ Coax the teacher into reading the teacher's manual with guided questions such as: "Tell me what you found helpful in this unit? What was your reaction to the story one of the groups will read next week? In what ways will you differentiate instruction for high achieving readers?"

Mentor: Supports the Teacher in Understanding the "What" and "Why"

New textbooks, especially in the content areas, from Grade 3 through high school could overwhelm the most veteran teacher. First, the bulk of them alone is intimidating. Then, the book (weighing at least 20 pounds each) comes accompanied by technology components, CDs, PowerPoint presentations, online worksheets, and so forth. Add to this an amazing array of information concerning the state's standardized testing portion of the text. What to use, what to lose, and what to do with what is there? A mentor could help.

♦ Assist by reviewing each of the teacher's manuals that accompany the instructional materials.

♦ Most new textbooks provide detailed instructions on what to do and how to do it. The mentor will help the novice learn how to manage and prioritize the most important components of the programs.

♦ Most new textbooks provide direct instruction for the teacher; including help in standardized test preparation. The mentor will demonstrate a system for adapting the information provided within the context of the classroom schedule.

♦ Assist or find someone to help implement the technology piece of an unfamiliar text component.

♦ Mentors provide the greatest resource for beginning teachers because they assist with the management aspect—the nuts and bolts. The mentor is the organized one; the one who demonstrates efficient systems for keeping track of student assessments, curriculum materials, and lesson plans.

◆ They provide the "what to do and when to do it" component that exists in the ever-increasing black cloud of paper, forms, and reports that frustrate even the veterans.

True Story

A veteran teacher volunteered to be my mentor during my first year teaching. She willingly shared all of her copies of seatwork with me (even though I was not quite sure what to do with all of them). She was so nice. She invited me to her house for dinner. She even gave me the calendar she used to plan her lessons, so I could also plan my activities for the year. In this way, I knew that the second week in March "we" make homemade butter.

—Elementary teacher (in Isaacson, 2005)

Leadership Opportunities

◆ Lead small group staff-development sessions. Apprentice-level teachers often contribute specific and innovative ideas to support the school goals. They train others in implementing a strategy that helps improve the performance of the teachers and the students.

◆ Represent the grade level or department at district-level curriculum meetings. The apprentice attends meetings that update existing information; this becomes new information to the apprentice-level teacher.

Often the school leader receives a memo from the district office that a school representative from each school must attend training to learn more about XYZ program or updates on a previous district mandate. This causes the leader to scramble to find anyone who appears vertical to drop everything and go. The master teacher often ends up representing the school. The master teacher has been there, done that, and usually does not want to relive the experience one more time.

The apprentice-level teacher will undoubtedly learn new information, shares the information in a positive way, and feels valued when asked to represent the school.

Up-Level Individual and Small Group Skills

◆ Find a group who wants to study student work samples. For example, examine what works, what doesn't, and how to improve student performance through changes in strategies.

- Identify one unit of instruction that occurs through the district-level guides such as an integrated conceptual unit or from the classroom textbook unit of study. Discuss implementation issues and concerns and how to fix them. Ask each other hard questions such as: What methods show us that all students understand the concept? What supplementary materials provide the most engaging approach for students to understand the concept?

- Examine individual data of students that appear common among the student group. Ask each other: What prevented student X from making improvement in reading from one year to the next? What strategies appear lacking in order for the student to improve at a higher rate? What interventions should we implement to support this student and others like him or her? What plan of action would benefit us, as a faculty group, with similar questions?

- Participation on strategic planning councils
  - As a school leader we identify subgroups who focus on specific issues and plans for improving student and teacher performance goals based on a global view of the school. Apprentice-level teachers fill these positions. It provides them the opportunity to up-level their skills through dialogue with problem-solving groups.

National Board Certification

Beginning the fourth year of effective teaching, the opportunity to engage in the rigorous and time-consuming process to become a Nationally Board Certified Teacher becomes an option for those interested. In 1987 the National Board for Professional Teaching Standards developed standards and certificates in more than 27 areas of instruction.

The application process requires several months to complete. This requires the creation of a portfolio that includes analyzing existing teaching strategies and opportunities for in-depth reflection on what occurs in the classroom. Video tapes and student work demonstrate the effect of teacher instruction. Supporting evidence includes the teacher's written reflections on their purposes of instruction, the results of their strategies, and commentaries on the rationale for their decisions. Teachers participating in the process also must include community and parent outreach.

A comprehensive portfolio provides a nationally assigned panel of readers the opportunity to judge the quality and effectiveness both in and out of the classroom, within the total school community. Once the portfolio is completed and sent to national assessment headquarters, one component remains. A four-hour written assessment requires candidates to respond in a narrative format to questions. Several months later, the results arrive.

Once a teacher "passes" the portfolio and written portions, financial remuneration becomes available, generally on two levels. States and districts provide different monetary amounts for passing. In addition, mentoring bonuses provide Nationally Board Certified Teachers compensation for mentoring and coaching the more inexperienced teachers. In many states the combined figures become a substantial increase in pay over the next 10 years.

The advantage for individual schools occurs when candidates are in the process of completing their portfolios. They become motivated to up-level their own teaching skills. The community outreach component provides the school leader with additional, competent staff members to assist with parent and community groups.

Since the comprehensive process requires each of the components for reflective inquiry into a teacher's instruction, knowledge of how students learn, curriculum understanding, and student assessment, it meets the criteria for effective personal staff development. If more than one teacher proceeds through the process during the year, this provides a quality team to work together and collaborate on effective classroom reflections. This becomes a highly individualized or differentiated approach.

The Leader's Role

Provide time for initial training with both mentors and coaches. It is possible to accomplish this task in an hour because we are working with experienced teachers who we already identified as competent.

- ◆ Provide agreed on times where the mentor and coach meet with the novice.
- ◆ Agree on the strategies and expectations concerning the role both people assume with the novice teacher.
- ◆ Recognize that not every teacher wants the responsibility or to take the time to mentor or coach. Not every teacher is good at it.
- ◆ Choose the best match possible. Volunteers are not always the most effective in this role.
- ◆ Establish a process to keep track of the apprentice group.
- ◆ Expect minutes from their group work; include the minutes as part of the documentation for each teacher's school plan.

- ♦ Those teachers who engage in the National Board Certification process require exceptional support from the school leader.
  - • Provide time for candidates to work together as part of their staff development.
  - • Find community and parent opportunities to fulfill that portion of their portfolio reflections.
  - • If other members of the staff already received their National Board Certification, they become mentors for those going through the process. They need time together.
  - • Once teachers receive their National Board Certification, provide a schoolwide ceremony—plaques, pictures, the works.
  - • National Board Certified teachers provide a positive public relations opportunity; take advantage of the "bragging rights" for press releases in the local and school papers.

Challenging the Master Teacher

As school leader, what can we do to challenge the master teacher? These are often the forgotten ones; often like gifted students. Just give them more work and they will be challenged. What assignments do master teachers often receive?

- ♦ Mentor the new teachers whether they want to or not—**more work.**
- ♦ Coach the struggling teachers—**more work.**
- ♦ Appointment to serve on committees where the teacher has no interest; often at the school site and district level—**more work**.
- ♦ By appointing them to the high status as "chairperson" of the same uninteresting committee—**more work.**
- ♦ Appointed to serve as team leader or department head—**more work.**

Although we may provide financial compensation attached to these add-on jobs; it is still more work for the teacher. As the school leader, do we assume that because the teacher accepts the job that they are interested or even want to do it? Although these jobs help the school run more smoothly, they do not challenge the master teacher. Then, what options become available?

First, every master teacher creates a specific plan to help implement the school goals. That is not challenging. They already know what to do and will continue.

The additional options for master teachers occur when each becomes part of the bigger picture. This group moves the school upward. They lead in a positive way in areas that interest them.

The initial meeting with master teachers invites a group of faculty members who meet criteria, such as the ones identified earlier, to meet as a group with the school leader. (If a veteran teacher believes he or she meets the criteria of a master teacher, [even if we don't think so], they still become part of the group as long as they contribute to the established goal.) At that time provide opportunities to discuss ways to move the school upward; advance the process of meeting the identified goals, yet, identify exemplary and innovative approaches.

The following ideas become discussion points from which to launch differentiated staff development for the master teachers. The same meeting structure becomes an option. This group can respond to the school leader's questions. "Where do we go from here? What should we anticipate?"

◆ Identify the possibilities for exploring new and innovative ideas.

◆ Set criteria for meeting schedules; expectations for reporting; criteria for presenting information, and to whom; timelines for completion.

◆ As leader we will determine the support available.

◆ As leader we identify our expectations; the teachers identify theirs.

The Master Teacher as New Program Change Agent

◆ As districts find new programs and resources to improve student performance, introductory information and the intent of the district to implement a "new idea" requires a district-level presentation. School-based representatives gather to listen to the new curricular decision. A master teacher can assimilate the information better than less experienced faculty members. They will process the ramifications more effectively. Many master teachers enjoy finding out about new programs and resources, especially if current practices need renovation. They could become part of a strategy team with the administrative support group if needed. Their staff development includes the effect of their participation at the district level with the existing staff.

◆ The administrative team recognizes that a change in programs, offerings, scheduling, or models will increase student progress. We ask a master teacher who understands the needs of students, the culture, and the importance of change to become part of our brainstorming and planning process. Throughout the year this teacher will provide

his/her positive influence with others when discussing the importance of the potential change.

Provide Model Classrooms

♦   Implementing school goals requires a model within the staff to demonstrate ways to meet those goals. For example, teachers agreed that
students need to learn to solve problems through creative, critical,
and conceptual thinking. One way of understanding how to implement this goal occurs when watching someone else engage students
in higher order questioning at a conceptual level. Master teachers
willingly open their doors for observations by others. The challenge
for master teachers happens when, as a result of being watched by a
colleague, they become even better at their craft, in this case, questioning techniques.

Trainer of Trainers

♦   Often district-level programs require implementation at the school-
sites. A "train-the-trainers" model usually accompanies the program.
Interested master teachers effectively serve that function. One problem: not every opportunity provided at a district level necessarily
focuses on the specific school goals. There is no point for a faculty
member to commit time and effort to a program or process that does
not directly affect the planned school goals. On the other hand, if
implementation will occur in the future, then the master teacher
takes on the role of the eventual change agent.

♦   Master teachers often provide the greatest resource for training their
colleagues. A team of teachers would develop a plan for small group
staff development and implement ways to identify strategies for staff
and student improvement.

When individuals become school-site "experts," they will study, plan, and
prepare to present to colleagues. This becomes an effective method for the
"expert's" individual goal.

Classroom Action Research

♦   Master teachers, along with mature apprentice faculty members,
who develop and implement classroom action research engage in
important and significant school-based research.

- Teachers identify a strategy or process they believe will improve student and teacher performance based on a school goal.
- Faculty members work with the school leaders and identify student data to support their efforts in finding more effective methods of instruction.
  - Teachers study the cause and effect relationships between the existing strategy and the answer to a guiding question.

The plan to learn effective classroom action research processes, the accompanying reflection, and continuous study of results constitute an effective individual or small group staff development for those involved. The process requires investigating the answer to a single, yet puzzling question.

When a group identifies classroom action research as their staff development, the following steps become the preliminary talking points:

Follow the data, both formal and informal assessments.

Identify a classroom problem; what is the question?

For example, based on a portion of classroom data, teachers generate a question: "When we do X, the results do not demonstrate our expectations for achievement. What could we do in a more effective way? Teachers could identify a splinter skill in reading. According to our standardized test and our individual assessments our higher level students are underperforming in the area of inferential reasoning. What are we doing now in class? What can we do in a different way?" Another example: "Students do not respond well to the higher-order questions that exist in the teacher's manual. What consistent strategies exist among the team for helping students make the critical conceptual connections? How can we improve our instruction to become more proficient at higher-order questioning? How will we know students are improving as we initiate new strategies? How will our plan connect to the schoolwide goals?"

As leader we would encourage more than one teacher to research a problem. In this way, collaboration and discussion provides the needed support to those examining an important issue. As long as the research question supports the school goal, a variety of research questions could exist simultaneously. For example, two teachers might examine a new approach to teaching inferential reasoning when reading in the social studies text (schoolwide goal: reading across the curriculum).

Four teachers might choose to research ways to provide higher-order questioning that focused on critical, creative, and conceptual thinking (schoolwide goal: students will learn to make decisions and solve problems through critical, creative, and conceptual thinking). Following this discussion, faculty members determine the focus.

♦ Develop and implement an action research plan (see Figure 6.1 for an example of a action research plan). Include the strategies for using and sharing the results.

Book Study, Focus, or Futurist Groups

As leader, another option occurs when we gather together the master level and interested apprentice teachers. This could occur after school since this group rarely whines about "the contract says ...". Given enough advanced warning, we should not have much trouble getting them together.

Whether a study, book, focus, or futurist group (and the group goals may overlap), the purpose remains the same. Gather together those with teaching experiences, motivation, and demonstrated success who begin planning for the school's long-range future.

Futurist Groups

Chapter 3 discussed a five-year plan with the administrative support team. The opportunity exists to bring them together with the futurist group. All of us brainstorm what the anticipated future holds and what role the school will play when meeting future demands from students. The group responds to the school leader's question: "As we talk to other teachers who demonstrate exceptional improvement with their students, and read about schools that create productive and innovative learning environments, what can we learn from them?"

A word of caution: On one hand, as school leader, we want this group to think "outside the box" and discuss possibilities without restraints. Stifling ideas becomes counterproductive to think-tank mentality. On the other hand, if there are known financial restraints, or issues that become beyond the scope of a reasonable expectation for success, reality does exist. For example, the futurists may agree that giving every student a laptop computer (or whatever technology may exist in the future) in a school with wireless Internet capabilities, ensures improvement in learning for all students. Yet, the school, built in 1920, requires several million dollars in renovation to accomplish this goal. Then what? As a futurist, the idea makes perfect sense, but, as a futurist in this specific environment, without a benevolent benefactor, it is impractical. It becomes a high-wire act for the administrator.

From this discussion, the group goes on a quest to learn about innovative and exemplary programs that have potential for them to explore and examine. Through a brainstorming process, the group may identify a common area to study. The end goal remains: What possible options, identified through the

Figure 6.1.

Individual Professional Development Plans

Teacher	Gr/ Dept	Topic	Meeting	Meeting	Meeting	Meeting

Differentiated Staff Development—Plan Meeting Notes

Teacher:	Topic:
Date of Meeting	
What is the status of your plan?	
Are you on schedule with your timeline? Why/Why not?	
What have you discovered about student learning?	
Do you have any resource needs?	

The second form could be on one or more sheets of paper and have dates for required numbers of meetings.

Classroom Action Research used with permission by Ralph Hewitt.

literature and research, could move the school upward? What would it look like, feel like, and sound like?

When an idea sounds possible, begin creating a plan to make it happen.

Study Groups

Futurist Extension

The discussion points identified in the Futurist Group now become study groups. The purpose: extensively explore the innovation identified during the futurist discussion. Determine the meeting site. Dates for meeting occur on the school calendar. Often, groups who enjoy the process meet at other times to dig deeper into their own learning.

The next step after identifying topics of interest during a brainstorming session requires finding information by locating other schools who successfully implemented the same idea with effective results.

One example: As school leader we become curious about a model for instruction that we believe may have possibilities for the school. We read about the enthusiasm for developing learning communities, yet, we are unfamiliar with the implementation. We mention this as an idea and see if two or more members of the group would be interested in further investigation. If so—great! If not, we may need another approach or drop the idea for now.

Research on the model begins. Different from classroom action research, this investigation requires finding other schools who achieved successful implementation of student and teacher performance based on futurist thinking. Group members decide the most logical references: Web sites; discussions with district-level experts; colleagues who implemented similar ideas; and current literature. Each member assumes a research responsibility. They return to the group during the next meeting and report their findings.

This group often requires at least a year-long investigation to determine the advantages, disadvantages, time-lines for implementation, and financial issues. This could ultimately mean a substantial change in the school's operation. Spend as much time as it takes before we make a final decision one way or the other. Examine all the options, including financial ones.

In-Depth Study of Strategies for Instruction

Teachers identify specific areas, based on the school goals, to improve existing practices. Strategies for implementing effective study groups include identifying roles for each member: recorder, host, and facilitator.

For example, the art, music, and physical education groups meet to identify reading strategies and methods for incorporating their areas of study with the school goal of reading across the curriculum. Or, this group may determine that a more important use of their time would address the goal of students learning to solve problems through creative, critical, and conceptual thinking.

Throughout the process, assigned reading occurs, based on the suggestions of the group. For example, music education journals address the critical connection between music and the application within the classroom. When the music teacher discusses his or her findings with the group it can spur other's ideas around the same conceptual thinking. Art education journals describe the integration of art and mathematical thinking. The art teacher could describe the content of his or her reading, provide the members of the study group with copies of the article and engage in a rich discussion that crosses disciplines and provides ideas for implementation.

Book Study

Often book study groups are an extension of colleagues' desires to improve a strategy currently used in connection with a school goal. In that sense it becomes similar to the in-depth study described above. In this case, the focus rests on a single book that identifies the strategies and ideas the group wants to investigate, try in their classrooms, and assess student progress using the specific guidance from a specific author. The identified author, generally suggested by a colleague, appears to provide a more effective approach in meeting the needs to improve reading instruction. For example, teachers who struggle with accommodating individual differences in their classrooms decide to focus on reading across the curriculum goal and choose work by Carol Ann Tomlinson and Jay McTighe (2006) on integrating and differentiated instruction or Amy Benjamin (2003) on differentiated instruction. Or, teachers interested in higher-order conceptual thinking that the district-level staff will soon introduce, will study the work of H. Lynn Erickson (2006) on concept-based thinking, and begin planning on ways to implement the approaches.

If the group is large enough, teachers identify different author's works with similar topics. Upon returning to the next meeting, faculty members compare likenesses and differences between the two. The groups identify strategies to incorporate in their individual classrooms, study the effects, assess improvement, and discuss the results.

The principal's role in supporting master teachers

♦ Participate with this group. They are the movers and shakers of the school organization and we, as the school leader, will become part of the thinking process that occurs within the group or groups.

♦ Help focus the master teachers' energies. Often, master teachers see issues from a variety of points of view. As a result, they may want to focus on too many tasks. Meet with this group and identify priorities. Depending on the numbers participating identify a reasonable number of issues on which to focus. Brainstorming options based on school goals could help us when gathering research, collecting and analyzing data, and drawing conclusions. We will guide faculty members as they identify the most important topics for a focus.

♦ If master teachers determine that new goals are required to up-level the existing school plan, then, as school leader we assist in creating a long-range plan to accomplish the identified recommendations. Based on the assessments, the administrative team and the master teacher groups identify fluid timelines.

♦ Data driven information determines the conditions and strategies that could support next year's school improvement plan focus. Members of our administrative support group should become part of this process in order to ensure continuity. The information and plan generated from this group could cycle back in upcoming years and become the discussion points and process identified and discussed beginning in chapter Two.

♦ This group, just as determined in all others, need time together.

♦ Provide a professional library on the identified topics that provide strategies, suggestions, Web site information, books, and articles. We, as the school leader, our administrative support group, the faculty problem-solving team, and those involved in their own staff development plan will suggest resources.

♦ It is up to us to find the money and to involve the media and technology specialists in the process of housing and cataloging resources for easy accessibility by the teachers.

♦ On the school calendar, identify times when sharing action research progress and findings occurs as part of schoolwide, department, or grade level.

The Special Needs Teachers

Some teachers do not fall into any of the categories mentioned earlier for a variety of reasons. What characteristics and developmental levels require special attention?

The faculty members referred to in this category do not fit the beginning teachers. Why? Very early in the first year of teaching, a conscientious mentor, coach, and focused observations by the school leaders, determines those who simply "don't fit into the school." Most districts allow for releasing this group from their contracts during a short probationary period. School districts also provide a more extended probationary status. This group falls into the zero-to two-year experience levels addressed earlier. Each of these faculty members receives support from a mentor and coach discussed earlier. At that time the staff members who demonstrate the skills, talents, and personal interaction to succeed in the school receives continued employment.

Third year teachers become problematic when their abilities fall in the "below expectation" level. This is their last year (in most districts) of their probationary status. Now what? The time is short before we must make a decision on their tenured position.

Staff development options become highly individualized and focused. Assign an administrative assistant, or assume the task ourselves, to develop a plan and closely monitor progress based on a tight set of criteria. The faculty member received support during the first two years; that didn't seem to work. Gather all the documentation collected during the previous years. (If we can meet with our administrative team during the summer to determine a strategic plan for the teacher, the time is well spent.) If not, meet with the mentor and coach to receive suggestions on a plan to determine the continued support for the teacher. Within the first two weeks of school, develop individualized development strategies with a strict focus and clear expectations.

Contrary to the literature concerning the importance of collaboration and democratic participation, situational leadership occurs under these conditions. In this case the staff member in question did not respond effectively to previous years with mentors and coaches in a way that we believe represents the expectations of quality instruction, assessment, and professional growth. The suggestions made by the previous support persons and our observations dictate the plan. Activities, assessments of students, how those assessments appear in documents (grade book, portfolio, etc.), additional observations, and continuous discussions with a supervisor become part of the expectations.

This sounds like a lot of work to salvage a teacher who does not naturally demonstrate competence. Regardless, two years is not much time for a teacher to develop all of the complexities of the craft, even at an "average" level. Continue other possibilities for support such as: (1) Providing another strong mentor and another strong coach; (2) if someone on our administrative support team comes from a background similar to the struggling teacher, assign the administrator as a coach; or (3) will a resource person at the county level provide ongoing assistance?

Differentiated staff development occurs from a single plan, with a single focus for one special needs teacher. Through continued feedback to the teacher and constant documentation, when it comes time to determine the decision on whether or not to rehire, the proof is in the data collected.

Another group, for whatever reason, obtained tenured status. The ineffective teacher in this group achieved this status on someone else's watch; certainly not ours. Regardless of the reason, we have decisions to make concerning the staff development options available to this teacher. Two different scenarios occur. If the faculty member gets along well with others, attempts to contribute to improving his or her craft (even if it is far removed from our beliefs) selecting the staff development plan that most fits his or her interest works. On the off-chance that the faculty member feels valued by participating with master teachers on a project, just maybe he or she will improve.

Tenured status teachers who do not get along well with others require a unique plan developed to find a niche for these teachers. An individual conference with one of us on the administrative team attempts a collaborative approach. Someone in this category generally does not see themselves the way others see them. They think everyone else "does not 'get it'." If they want to become part of forward-thinking groups of master teachers, beware. They will sabotage the group.

If we are a very brave principal, we tell the ineffective veteran teacher that, because we promote differentiated staff development; they will develop an individual plan (under our strict criteria for results and based on hard data). They will show results for themselves and the students based on clear expectations. As school leader, we should be the one to work with these faculty members.

Under some circumstances, tenured, ineffective teachers often learn something by serving on writing teams. They usually have history with the existing curriculum and could help others understand how concepts and strategies evolved. Make sure a strong master teacher, or an administrator facilitates the group.

A more difficult decision occurs when thinking of the old adage: "Do we want to spend 90% of our time on 10% of the people" (who don't or won't "get it")? Choices made for that group require insight and determination on the strategies for differentiated staff development.

Small Groups That Combine Mixed Developmental Levels

One common reason for combining mixed developmental levels for small groups occurs when the curriculum for a grade level or department requires review, discussion, and possible changes or modification. For example, the existing curriculum, instruction, and assessment do not address the school goals for all teachers. The school goal of reading across the curriculum occurs clearly in the teacher's manual and resources for the teachers of reading, but not for every other subject area. Although the support area teachers of art, music, and physical education, created their differentiated staff development plan as a small group, the rest of the content area teachers do not know their plan. Regardless of the developmental level of each faculty member, everyone should become part of the process to create a curriculum map so everyone who works with the same students, understand each other's ideas and plans for implementation of reading across the curriculum.

School Goals for Select Teachers

Horizontal and Vertical Teams or Departments

As school leader, we provide all levels of teachers the opportunity to participate in horizontal team or department meetings. Our presence maintains the focus and prevents any individual from detracting from the purpose of the identified task.

Staff development created among horizontal teams provides meaningful opportunities to examine the existing curriculum, instruction, and assessment for continuity within a team or department. Vertical teams focus on a continuum of learning experiences from one grade to the next.

Either group could examine whether or not "holes" exist in the grade level or department curriculum. This exists with the implementation of a new program, the creation of new standards, or specific areas on standardized testing that demonstrates a weakness in the curriculum and instruction in a particular subtest.

If there are holes in the curriculum, it is likely that the instructional materials do not provide the resources. The decision on how best to fill the holes could be assigned to a subcommittee to investigate and later make recommendations. In this way the days are spent in the productive activity of curriculum development; not thumbing through catalogues.

In addition to the holes that exist, the team may realize that they are either overteaching or underteaching some concepts. Textbooks may contain content that, because "it is there," teachers feel compelled to teach "it" whether students need it or not. Or, teachers will argue that they always taught "it" and students should know it "just because." This discussion lends itself well to the discussion and decision making on several instructional issues:

- ♦ Time
  - Quality time spent on the critical content; too much, too little?
  - What is the expected time frame needed to teach this area of study?
- ♦ Strategies
  - When ideas and suggestions are generated from this group, it becomes necessary to embed instructional strategies into the cur-

riculum design. Members of the administrative team help develop a plan that answers the question: How will the recommendations translate into the classroom to meet the school goal of "reading across the curriculum as students learn to solve problems, make decisions, and think critically?"

- Times change and instructional materials become antiquated. As teams discuss effective use of strategies, and purposeful instruction, thoughtful dialogue should produce recommendations to eliminate some past practices as new ideas and materials become available. Emphasis on the most effective materials and strategies should supersede arguments over the value of outdated instructional methods and materials.

- Are the instructional strategies purposeful in order to adapt to the needs of the students? How are those needs being identified and recorded?

For an example of a planning grid, see Figure 6.2 on page 131.

Staff Development Options

Planning Time for One or Two Days

Providing time for teachers to plan, away from the students, was discussed earlier. Experienced principals recognize the advantages of getting team members together to examine existing practices for purposes of improving curriculum, instruction, and assessment. The quality of the process results in a product where every member of the group takes ownership. No one should be left out of the opportunity to learn, discuss, and plan together in a collaborative environment.

There are different groupings that become possible, depending on the area of need. Problem solving and decision making can occur by vertical teams (all teachers of science—remember we are targeting reading across the curriculum) horizontal, (all fifth grade teachers), self-contained instructional groups of students (teachers of non-English speaking; exceptional education; physical education; art; music). We may choose to include teachers of self-contained groups among the other teams, not as a separate group.

It doesn't matter as long as they are included in the entire process. Whatever group we choose, anyone left out of the process will not understand what they are supposed to do, and why the decisions were made to "do it that way."

Figure 6.2.

Vision:

Mission:

Goals:

Grade level or team _____

Curricular area of study _____

Standard	Primary Text and Materials Used	Time Frame for Instruction	Classroom Assessment Used	State and National Test Score for the Standard
ABC.1	Textbook, 123, ch. 4 Video tape "Y"	2 instructional days	Essay on the subject of "Y" comparing text-book discussions and video	Not tested
ABC. 2	Not taught	—	—	Level 1 = X# 2 = X# 3 = X# 4 = X#
No Standard— Teachers think this is an important concept because …	Textbook, 123, ch 8	5 days	Teams are judged in a debate based on ch. 8	Not tested

Left up to the teacher to "volunteer" to be away from the classroom, often they won't come. Not because they don't want to, but because they say they would rather be with their students. As school leader, we explain the importance of the process. It becomes as expectation.

Beyond Curriculum Alignment

An example of a complex task that requires one or two days for a whole team follows. During discussions with teachers, we believe that students seem unprepared from one grade to the next in the area of expository reading and writing.

The hypothesis exists, that somewhere in the curriculum, every teacher thinks that instruction occurs with someone else. We gather a team to identify the problem and possibly unearth other inconsistencies in the language arts strands of the existing program. We may choose this activity for small segments of time with groups of teachers before meeting as a full team. In this way we will maximize the time to focus on the instructional component during a full day of examining the language arts curriculum.

A group could form to create a curriculum map. Perhaps the instructional materials do not provide the resources. The decision on how best to resolve curriculum conflicts that surfaced become assigned to a subcommittee to investigate and later make recommendations. In this way the days are spent in the productive activity of curriculum development, not thumbing through catalogues to find more materials.

In studying the overall curriculum map, the team may realize that they are either overteaching or underteaching some concepts. Again, textbooks may contain content that, because "it is there," teachers feel compelled to teach "it" whether students need it or not. Or, teachers will argue that they always taught "it" and students should know it "just because." This discussion lends itself well to the discussion and decision making on several instructional issues:

The Leader's Role

Before, During, and After a Team Planning Meeting

- ♦ Before:
  - Meet with the problem-solving team to determine the areas of focus.

- Identify the team; vertical, horizontal, or both groups meeting at different times.
  - This involves everyone serving on both groups, but for different purposes, and at different times.
- Plan the details of the meeting with the administrative support group

  Questions to the small group:
- Did we find that the standardized test required knowledge for which the students did not have the background to answer?
- Is this a realistic and developmentally appropriate skill or concept? Is there a prerequisite skill or concept missing? What is it?

- During the meeting
  - Keep the issues focused.
  - Identify weaknesses in the existing curriculum based on lack of continuity in skill development.
  - Resolve the questions: How far can we take our students based on (1) developmentally appropriate skills; (2) understanding the depth of content; and (3) application to "enduring understandings" (Erickson, 2006; Tomlinson & McTighe, 2006; Wiggins & McTighe (1999).
  - Determine the expectations for accomplishing grade level standards through purposeful instruction (Benjamin, 2003; Northey, 2005; Tomlinson & McTighe, 2006).
  - Are there areas on the standardized testing subtests that indicate "holes exist" in the current instruction or curriculum? Provide a type of frame in the example above.
  - Assign someone to record the discussion.
  - Identify ways to display the issues such as on chart paper.

- After the meeting
  - Provide minutes to the team for any revisions needed.
  - Provide the final document (based on the meeting's decisions).
  - Present the key points from the meeting at a general staff meeting.
  - Utilize these decisions to guide future meetings with additional teams.

- Create a process to observe teachers as they implement the area of study they designed. In this way they know we are serious about the product they created and the value we place on their work.

Possible scenarios exist for identifying which of the options faculty members select to implement. Although, as school leaders, we hope teachers would select from a menu of options (the ones we would also identify, although this isn't always the case). Under what circumstances would the options become a teacher's choice, and which options becomes the school leader's choice?

School Leader's Choice

The district-level staff makes a decision to implement a new program. For example, the district curriculum team announced they will write concept-based thematic units; they will be field-tested during the upcoming year. A member or members of the staff will be selected to serve on the writing team. We make the most logical selection. We know the people or person who possesses the skills and talents to provide meaningful insight into the writing.

We ask the person (usually a master teacher) who would view the experience as an opportunity for professional growth. We make an agreement that the selection assumes this person becomes the "on-site" trainer upon the completion of the units.

In this case we determine that the complex nature of the task, the learning that will occur as a result, this is the staff development plan the teacher will create. It has a direct connection to the schoolwide goal.

During the field-testing year those members of the writing team will implement the units, and begin discussing the program with their colleagues. (Since the first year of field testing will not provide direct data for student improvement, this still meets the school leader's criteria for personal professional growth for the teachers involved.)

This example also illustrates a time when a principal intervenes in imposing an individual or small group goal.

Earlier in the discussions student tardiness became a talking point during the schoolwide planning meeting. At that time our team determined that it did not affect every teacher. However, we know it is still a problem. The intervention and plans are handled differently with a small group than with the school as a whole.

Our administrative team discussed the concern and determined it was more than students not getting to class on time. After the facts are investigated, it reveals that the problem reflects on individual teachers.

Students show up late in some individual teachers' classrooms more than others. A member of our administrative team is assigned the responsibility of using their problem-solving training to develop goals and strategies to "get the students to class on time." Only those teachers where there appears a concern meet to discuss the issues, concerns, and ideas for solutions.

- Meet with those involved and utilize the problem-solving strategy to arrive at ways to implement ideas.
- Prepare and present the hard data.
- Discuss the issues with the teachers.
  - Examine unique situations that occur. The problem may not rest with the teacher, but rather other extenuating circumstances.
  - If data can support individual teacher problems as the cause of student tardiness then those teachers remain to discuss solutions.
- Facilitate the creation of goals and strategies.
- Develop a monitoring system.
- Assign a member of the team who is responsible for reporting weekly progress.

Goal:

We will decrease the number of student tardiness—(when?) At the beginning of each class period by 80% by May of (year). Monthly monitoring will be provided by each teacher to the assistant principal. Follow-up meetings will occur if the goal is below expectation.

Teachers:
Listed:

- The administrative team member asks probing questions to arrive at strategies or activities to meet the goals such as:
  - How will we get students to value coming to class on time?
  - Identify the specific details on the first 10 minutes of the class where the student is missing part of that time.

- ♦ The administrative team member will:
  - Arrange and facilitate the meeting.
  - Provide minutes of each meeting to the rest of the faculty and we, the leader, immediately following the discussion.
  - Continue the process that includes strategies and timelines for completing assigned tasks.
  - Build consensus on a method of final accountability.
  - Identify someone to edit the draft.
  - Provide the administrator with a rough draft.
  - Create a final draft.
  - Place the plan into the final document.

This example demonstrates the need to create staff development based on the needs of the school as a whole as well. In most cases, this does not require the involvement of everyone. The identified problem becomes part of the individual teacher's staff development plan.

Questions and Answers

Q: What is the difference in the tasks between a vertical team and a horizontal one?

A: Vertical teams effectively identify the continuum on which content develops from one grade level to the next. Expectations of student achievement provide indicators teachers use to discuss the optimum depth and breadth of understanding a student could accomplish from one grade level to the next. Vertical teams find the holes in the curriculum easier than a horizontal team.

Q: If teachers serve on committees or participate in things like focus groups, how could they make the connection between that activity and improved test scores for their students?

A: As a school leader, refocus on the purpose everyone serves. If the district accepts only teacher goals based on specific improvement on a standardized test score, then limit the number of goals. The additional goal is generated at the school site and becomes differentiated based on the teacher's ability to contribute to the overall success of adults. One goal meets a district requirement; the other goal meets the specific needs addressed by the leadership groups.

Q: In a time when finding teachers become very difficult, I am reluctant to dismiss a slightly below-average teacher. I worry that someone that takes his or her place will not be any better. Then, I have to start all over again.

A: This is a moral decision. The given in this case occurs when we know a teacher is below average. What does that tell us about how a below-average teacher affects rooms of students? The long-range affect on a student with a poor teacher is significant. Do we want a below-average school? Universities still produce excellent potential teachers.

Q: Why involve only mature apprentice and master teachers in action research? Why not everyone?

A: Mature apprentice and master teachers generally understand underlying issues that require significant investigation with the classroom. They ask the hard "why" questions concerning lack of expected student performance. They express a desire to figure out how to improve existing practices or try new ideas. All other groups of teachers still concentrate on demonstrating foundational instructional and assessment strategies.

Q: If the school needs a faculty member to participate in a specific professional development task, why not just ask for volunteers? Why should I, as the school leader, take the time to identify specific individuals?

A: Mature apprentice and master-level teachers have the knowledge base and experience to see the big picture. As a result, they bring to the table quality insight into the task. They also understand the existing school culture, so that on completion they know the best way to present the information to the staff members.

Q: As the school leader, how can I keep track of each staff member's goals?

A: Create a schoolwide calendar that identifies each date identified as nonnegotiable. This includes any dates the district and/or we provide for schoolwide staff development. Since differentiated staff development occurs the identified dates demonstrate to the faculty that time set aside means that each person meets with their identified groups based on common goals. When faculty members identify their goals, the meeting dates become part of the plan that we receive. The staff member's goals become part of our school calendar. Figure 6.3 on p. 138 provides an example of a calendar.

Figure 6.3.

The School Leader's Differentiated Staff Development Calendar

How does a school leader keep track of everyone; their differentiated staff development goal? Organized principals often keep a binder with information concisely identified. The following example becomes one piece of documentation for you.

One method: a spread sheet. The point: without a system to keep track of what you are expecting of faculty members in order to meet the schoolwide mission and purpose, values, and schoolwide goals you assume "facts not in evidence."

Teacher's Name by Grade Level or Department	Goal Identified	Meeting Dates to Review Goals With Me	Aug.	Sept.	Oct.	Etc.
(secretaries can prepare this column)	When the goals are completed, you will enter the dates when you or a member of your administrative support will meet for individual review of teacher progress.)					

Survival Tips

- *Eliminate extraneous staff development sessions.* An idea that we think important to present to the schoolwide staff that has nothing to do with the agreed-upon goals fragments the schoolwide goals focus. Hold that thought for a time when the concept matches the goal.

- *Provide time for mentors and coaches to meet together with their novice teachers.* Coaches and their novice teachers need extra time together. Find a way to make it happen. This is the time to get creative in finding time that is not perceived as an intrusion on teacher's planning time. Some schools set up a breakfast club when all novice teachers and their mentors and coaches gather to describe common issues and concerns. The school leader provides a continental breakfast, and joins the group to lend support.

  Others find business partners who provide coupons for free lunch. The entire group gets together after school for discussion. (A key facilitator in the group keeps the focus on support for the novice.)

  Establish a tracking and monitoring system so that, in the hectic pace of the year, this group does not eventually "forget or can not find time to meet." Then at the end of the year the novice announces that "no one ever told me ..."

- *Keep the development plan for the novice simple.* Often, small groups will determine similar goals and strategies to achieve them, based on prior experiences and background knowledge. The coach helps the novice recognize the realistic expectations. The goal for a beginning teacher may become one of learning the existing curriculum with specific emphasis on one schoolwide goal. Reading across the curriculum requires learning to understand the teacher's manuals.

- *Develop a system to keep track of teacher's development plans.* In large schools, principals and assistants need help to keep track of the progress of individual faculty members. It is not uncommon for school leaders to start the year effectively keeping track of individual's goals, and then forget who is doing what.

- *Put time and money into staff development decisions.* Faculty members do not have the energy to consistently work on staff development after school. Time to think together and plan together within the school day becomes the most valuable support a leader provides.

♦ *Dedicate time for members of the administrative support team to participate with differentiated staff development groups.* A variety of positive effects exist when an administrator becomes part of staff groups. It works both ways. The teachers see their leaders placing value in what they do. The administrator learns from the faculty members as they discuss the issues and create strategies to improve their own and student learning. Together, they keep a focus on doing the right thing, in the best way possible.

♦ *During the first staff development meeting, make sure the facilitator knows the expectation that teachers will complete their individual plan at that time.* The school calendar will provide assigned dates for staff development meetings. However, the group may decide on other times to include. The facilitator will collect the completed plans and submit them to the principal.

♦ *Identify specific days on our calendar, and the calendars of administrative team for goal reflection with the members of the faculty to whom everyone is responsible.* Once we receive the individual goals, and identify staff development options, mark our calendar. In the hectic schedules of the year, it is easy to place goal review as a low priority. Our administrative team could meet during the required time and still assign a member of the problem-solving team to help out.

Summary

Differentiated staff development provides advantages from a variety of perspectives. It meets all the needs of the school, the diverse groups of staff members, and teacher and student expectations for continued improvement.

Individual differences and needs among the staff and students require a reexamination of school-site staff development. Even if a new program or approach to student learning becomes the goal of the school, individuals and groups view their particular role in achieving that goal in different ways.

Understanding the basic elements of a new program, textbook, or strategy requires realistic expectations on the part of the leader regarding the developmental levels of teachers. Information overload becomes one of the more common frustrations of new teachers. They try to take it all in, figure out how to make it work, and become overwhelmed. Assign mentors and coaches who work with novice teachers throughout all three years. Staff development for the first three years should involve individualized support.

Formal plans would include small incremental steps on the path toward meeting schoolwide goals.

Throughout the process of identifying teacher's learning, the fundamental issues of working within the school community must continuously focus on the identified school goals. Individuals improve their learning experiences when remaining steadfast to the mission, vision, values, and schoolwide goals through the lenses of moral and ethical leadership.

When school leaders provide the opportunity for differentiated staff development based upon schoolwide goals, they provide a focus. The purpose and mission become demonstrated when faculty members meet in small groups and continue to reinforce a common belief. This vision, based on the one created by the entire faculty, sets the tone for each member's purpose.

Both theory and research indicate that teachers learn better in teams. It becomes the moral imperative for school leaders to provide a platform on which teachers study improved methods of curriculum, instruction, and assessment.

Additional advantages of small group interaction with a single purpose occur. Relationships form when those involved interact through the lenses of moral and ethical leadership. Faculty members make decisions based on their moral, ethical, and purposeful beliefs about the best ways to serve the students. At the same time, teachers interact with each other based on the values shared that student improvement exists when their individual curriculum, instruction, and assessment skills and knowledge improves.

Application

- ♦ How would moral, ethical, and purposeful beliefs affect decisions when faculty members work together to create a plan for their personal development and student achievement?
- ♦ What different attitudes, behaviors, and commitments might a novice, an apprentice, special needs, or a master teacher make when identifying the importance of learning to implement a new program through the perspective of individual values?
- ♦ What are the advantages of utilizing a differentiated staff development model for the staff?
- ♦ What are the advantages and disadvantages of a differentiated staff development model for the administrators?
- ♦ Discuss the moral and ethical implications when developing a differentiated staff development model.

- Discuss how this model fits into the need for teachers to commit to the mission, vision, values, and schoolwide goal.
- Would we associate the differentiated staff development model with a purposeful leader? Why or why not?

"When we do things from a moral imperative, living truthfully becomes fundamental to our way of living, as we don't give up because of short-term setbacks."

—Ghandi (in Nair, 1997)

Final Thoughts

Building a community by creating a family environment requires a commitment by all stakeholders to pull together and provide teachers, students and parents with the most effective learning environment possible.

When identifying the key issues that make a school even better than great—fantastic, the following messages may help:

- Know yourself, who you are, and what exactly your job purpose is.
- Gather trusted support people around you.
- Nurture, support, and challenge your staff.
- Recognize and respond to individual differences.
- Keep focused.
- Build, reflect, discuss, and solve problems together.

School leaders no longer work in isolation. The job of an administrator is too complex. Some principals lead schools with a population larger than most small towns. You can not do it alone. Building a community by creating a family environment requires a commitment by all stakeholders to pull together and provide teachers, students and parents with the most effective learning environment possible.

A moral, ethical, and purposeful school leader will:

1. Think beyond the high-stakes fetish as a stand alone component of learning.

2. Understand the complex nature of working with individual staff members in order to raise expectations for instruction beyond the traditional approach to student learning.

3. Listen to teachers. The ones who think about student progress, or lack of it, and wonder why.

4. Examine how teachers figure out more effective ways to help students progress along a developmental continuum.

5. Listen to teachers who struggle and ask, "What will it take to help you feel more successful?" Then, do what it takes to support them.

6. Know the thinkers. They spend time digging deeply into their own personal beliefs. They examine their own vision for the teachers and students. They keep asking the "why" questions.

7. Know themselves and the purpose for which they work with teachers, students, and families.

8. Learn curriculum for which they have no personal experience, in order to understand the issues raised by each teacher.

9. Manage when they have to (often on the run); they are visibly the instructional leader all the time the students and teachers are together.

10. Attend each staff development training session designed to bring the philosophy and vision of the teachers to fruition. They stay the course.

11. They see every person in the school as individuals with specific needs, strengths, and interests as they differentiate staff development.

"The rung of a ladder was never meant to rest upon but only to hold a man's foot long enough to enable him to put the other somewhat higher."

—Thomas Henry Huxley

Appendix

Mission, Vision, Values, and Goals Through the Lenses of Moral, Ethical, and Purposeful Leadership

Moral behavior is a result of our personal and cultural experiences. Morals are exhibited through:

- Fairness
- Honesty
- Promise Keeping
- Truth Telling
- Justice
- Equality
- Tolerance
- Responsibility
- Do to others what you want done to you.

Ethical behavior is a result of our professional and societal values and based on principles, beliefs, and virtues that constitute a moral life. Ethics is exhibited through:

- Integrity
- Loyalty
- Kindness
- Courage
- Generosity
- Compassion
- Unselfishness

Values are guided by our moral compass. Values are exhibited by what we feel and what we do. Values statements answer a question. What attitudes, behaviors, and commitments will drive our school?

Purpose is driven by our passion for why we are here.

Mission statements answer a question. What is our school's purpose?

Vision statements answer a question. Where are we going?

Goal statements answer questions. What steps are necessary to get there? How will we know if and when we accomplished our goals?

References and Other Source Material

Adler, R., & Elmhorst, J. M. (2005). *Communication at work: Principles and practices for business and the professions* (8th ed.). Boston: McGraw-Hill.

Alvy, H. B., & Robbins, P. (1998). *If I only knew: Success strategies for navigating the principalship.* Thousand Oaks, CA: Corwin Press.

Barth, R. S. (1990). *Improving schools from within: Teachers, parents, and principals can make a difference.* San Francisco: Jossey-Bass.

Barth, R. S. (2001). *Learning by heart.* San Francisco: Jossey-Bass.

Beckner, W. (2004). *Ethics for educational leaders.* Boston: Pearson.

Beck. L. G., & Murphy, J. (1994). *Ethics in educational leadership programs: An expanding role.* Thousand Oaks, CA: Corwin Press.

Becker, W. (2004). *Ethics for educational leaders.* Boston: Pearson.

Benjamin, A. (2003). *Differentiated instruction: A guide for elementary school teachers.* Larchmont, NY: Eye on Education.

Bennis, W. (1989). *On becoming a leader.* Reading MA: Addison-Wesley.

benShea, N. (2000). *What every principal would like to say ... and what to say next time: Quotations for leading, learning, and living.* Thousand Oaks, CA: Corwin Press.

Birchak, B., Connor, C., Crawford, K. M., Kahn, L., Kaser, S., Turner, S., et al. (1998). *Teacher study groups: Building community through dialogue and reflection.* Urbana, IL: National Council of Teachers of English.

Blase, J., & Blase, J. (1998). *Handbook of instructional leadership: How really good principals promote teaching and Learning.* Thousand Oaks, CA: Corwin Press.

Blase, J., & Blase, J. (2003). *Breaking the silence: Overcoming the problem of principal mistreatment of teachers*. Thousand Oaks, CA: Corwin Press.

Bordas, J. (1995). *Power and passion: Finding personal purpose*. In L. Spears (Ed.), *Reflections on leadership: How Robert K. Greenleaf's theory of servant leadership influenced today's top management thinkers* (pp. 179-193). New York: Wiley.

Brown, J. L., & Moffett, C. A. (1999). *The hero's journey: How educators can transform schools and improve learning*. Alexandria, VA: Association for Supervision and Curriculum Development.

Calabrese, R. L. (2000). *Leadership through excellence: Professional growth for school leaders*. Boston: Allyn & Bacon.

Caine, R. N., & Caine, G. (1997). *Education on the edge of possibility*. Alexandria, VA: Association for Supervision and Curriculum Development.

Carr, J. F., & Harris, D. E. (2001). *Succeeding with standards: Linking curriculum assessment, and action planning*. Alexandria, VA: Association for Supervision and Curriculum Development.

Cheyney, A. B. (1998). *People of purpose: 80 people who have made a difference*. Glenview, IL: Good Year Books.

Ciulla, J. B. (2005). Introduction. In J. B. Ciullo, T. L. Price, & S. E. Murphy (Eds.), *The quest for moral leadership* (pp. 1-9). Cheltenham, United Kingdom: Edward Elgar.

Ciulla, J. B., Price, T. L., & Murphy, S. E. (2005). *The quest for moral leaders: Essays on leadership ethics*. Cheltenham, United Kingdom: Edward Elgar.

Collins, J. (2001). *Good to great*. New York: HarperCollins.

Czaja, M., Fisher, A., & Hutton, N. (2001). *Ethics: A major challenge for the 21st century*. Paper presented at the Texas Professors of Educational Administration Fall Meeting, Austin, TX.

Champy, J. (1995). *Reengineering management*. New York: HarperCollins.

Combs, A. W., Miser, A. B., & Whitaker, K. S. (1999). *On becoming a school leader: A person-centered challenge*. Alexandria, VA: Association of Supervision and Curriculum Development.

Cook, S. D. (2005). That which governs best: leadership, ethics, and human systems. In J. B. Ciullo, T. L. Price, & S. E. Murphy (Eds.), *The quest for moral leaders: Essays on leadership ethics* (pp. 131-143). Northampton, MA: Edward Elgar.

Cotton, K. (2003). *Principals and students achievement: What the research says*. Alexandria, VA: Association for Supervision and Curriculum Development.

Covey, S. R. (1990). *Seven habits of highly effective people*. New York: Simon & Schuster.

Covey, S. R. (1991). *Principle-centered leadership*. New York: Simon & Schuster.

Daft, R. L., & Lengel R. H. (2000). *Fusion leadership: Unlocking the subtle forces that change people and organizations.* San Francisco: Berrett-Koehler.

Darling-Hammond, L. (1997). *The right to learn: A blueprint for creating schools that work.* San Francisco: Jossey-Bass.

Deal T. E., & Peterson, K. D. (1999). *Shaping school culture: The heart of leadership.* San Francisco: Jossey-Bass.

Donaldson, G. A. (2001). *Cultivating leadership in schools: Connecting people, purpose, and practice.* New York: Teachers College Press.

Dubrin, A. J. (2004). *Leadership: Research findings, practice, and skills* (4th ed.). Boston: Houghton Mifflin.

DuFour R. (1991). *The principal as staff developer.* Bloomington, IN: National Education Service.

DuFour R., & Eaker, R. (1998). *Professional learning communities at work: Best practices for enhancing student achievement.* Bloomington, IN: National Educational Service.

Dembowski, F. L., & Lemaster, L. K. (Eds.). *The 2006 yearbook of the national council of professors of educational administration.* Lancaster, PA: DEStech Publications.

Edmonson, S., & Fisher, A. (2006). Ethics in principal preparation programs: A move towards best practice. In F. L. Dembowski & L. K. Lemasters (Eds.), *Unbridled spirit: Best practices in educational administration* (pp. 182-189). Lancaster, PA: DEStech Publications.

Elmore, R. (2000). *Building a new structure for school leadership.* Washington, DC: Albert Shanker Institute.

Erickson, H. L. (2001). *Stirring the head, heart, and soul* (2nd ed.). Thousand Oaks, CA: Corwin Press.

Erickson, H. L. (2006). *Concept-based curriculum and instruction for the thinking classroom.* Thousand Oaks, CA: Corwin Press.

Evans, R. (1996). *The human side of school change: Reform, resistance, and the real-life problems of innovation.* San Francisco: Jossey-Bass.

Fleck, F. (2005). *What successful principal do! 169 tips for principals.* Larchmont, NY: Eye on Education.

Fiore, D. J. (2004). *Introduction to educational administration: Standards, theories, and practice.* Larchmont, NY: Eye on Education.

Fiore, D. J., & Joseph C. (2005). *Making the right decisions: A guide for school leaders.* Larchmont, NY: Eye on Education.

Fullan, M. (Ed.). (1997). *The challenge of school change.* Arlington Heights, IL: Skylight Professional Development.

Glatthorn, A. A. (2000). *The principal as curriculum leader: Shaping what is taught & tested* (2nd ed.). Thousand Oaks, CA: Corwin Press.

Glickman, C. D. (2002). *Leadership for learning: How to help teachers succeed.* Alexandria, VA: Association for Supervision and Curriculum Development.

Green, L. R. (2005). *Practicing the art of leadership: A problem-based approach to implementing the ISLLC standards* (2nd ed.). Upper Saddle River, NJ: Pearson-Merrill-Prentice Hall.

Greenleaf, R. K. (1977). *Servant leadership.* New York: Paulist Press

Guskey, T. (1999). Apply time with wisdom. *Journal of Staff Development, 20*(2), 10-14.

Guskey, T. R. (2000). *Evaluating professional development.* Thousand Oaks, CA: Corwin Press.

Haynes, F. (1998). *The ethical school.* New York: Routledge.

Heller, D. A. (2004). *Teachers wanted: Attracting and retaining good teachers.* Alexandria, VA: Association for Supervision and Curriculum Development.

Isaacson, L. (2005). *Smart, fast, efficient: The new principal's guide to success.* Larchmont, NY: Eye on Education.

Jacobs, H. H. (Ed.). (2004). *Getting results with curriculum mapping.* Alexandria, VA: Association for Supervision and Curriculum Development.

Kellerman, B. (2005). Leadership: Warts and all. *Harvard Business Review,* p. 13.

Kidder, R. M. (1995). *How good people make tough choices.* New York: William Morrow.

Kopeikina, L. *The right decision every time: How to reach perfect clarity on tough decisions.* Upper Saddle River, NJ: Pearson-Prentice Hall.

Kouzes, J. M., & Posner, B. Z. (1987). *The leadership challenge: How to get extraordinary things done in organizations.* San Francisco: Jossey-Bass.

Kouzes, J. M., & Posner, B.Z. (1993). *Credibility: How leaders gain and lose it, why people demand it.* San Francisco: Jossey-Bass.

MacIntyre, A. (1966). *A short history of ethics.* New York: Macmillan.

McEwan, E. K. (2003). *10 traits of highly effective principals: From good to great performance.* Thousand Oaks, CA. Corwin Press.

Manz, C. C., & Sims, H. P. (2001). *The new superleadership: Leading others to lead themselves.* San Francisco: Berrett-Koehler.

Marzano, R. J. (2003). *What works in schools: Translating research into action.* Alexandria, VA: Association for Supervision and Curriculum Development.

Marzano, R. J., Waters, T., & McNulty, B. A. (2005). School leadership that works: From research to results. Alexandria, VA: Association for Supervision and Curriculum Development.

Maxwell, J. C. (1995). *Developing the leaders around you: How to help others reach their full potential.* Nashville, TN: Thomas Nelson.

Maxwell, J. C. (2001). *The 17 indisputable laws of teamwork: Embrace them and empower your team.* Nashville, TN: Thomas Nelson.

Mother Teresa quotes. Retrieved April 2, 2007, from http://en.thinkexist.com, quotes/mother_teresa_of_calcutta

Nair, K. (1997). *A higher standard of leadership: Lesson from the life of Gandhi.* San Francisco: Berrett-Koehler.